tual history has been the hope of the European immigrants in coming to the New World: they could there undergo a religious experience of rebirth which would allow them to transcend the tension of the historical communities of the Old World. Our novels have convinced me that this tension is inevitable because the human community must always have roots in the past even as it must have a vision of the future.

"Since I am a historian, my first recognition of the attempt by modern Americans to escape the problem of time found expression in the analysis of our historical writings. But it is also possible to suggest that our novels, because they deal with the history of an individual or a group of individuals, have forced their authors always to confront and often to criticize the central myth of our civilization—the transcendence of time."

*David W. Noble,* Professor of History at the University of Minnesota, is the author of *The Paradox of Progressive Thought* and *Historians Against History.*

# The Eternal Adam
## and the
## New World Garden

*Also by David W. Noble*

THE PARADOX OF PROGRESSIVE THOUGHT

HISTORIANS AGAINST HISTORY
*The Frontier Thesis and the National Covenant
in American Historical Writing Since 1830*

# The Eternal Adam
## and the
# New World Garden

---

*The Central Myth in the*
*American Novel Since 1830*

---

## DAVID W. NOBLE

*George Braziller*
NEW YORK

*For David and Becky,*

*Jeffrey, Douglas, and Patricia*

# Acknowledgments

In my previous books I have acknowledged my indebtedness to a community of scholars in American cultural history. Many I have mentioned by name, many others are not so identified. I believe every human enterprise is an expression of human interdepedence. I am grateful to all those scholars who have forged the rich tradition on which I have depended in making my particular synthesis. Now I would like to thank especially the literary critics, Leslie Fiedler, Henry Nash Smith, and Lionel Trilling, whose writings played a crucial role at the beginning of the 1950's in ending my loyalty to what I call the "Puritan tradition" in the writing of American history. In its place, they taught me to recognize the magnificent richness of tradition expressed in the American novel. I would also like to thank those from whose writings I have borrowed most directly: Roger Salomon and his book, *Twain and the Image of History,* and Robert Schneider and his book, *Five Novelists of the Progressive Era.* I am also indebted to two graduate students at the University of Minnesota from whose unpublished papers I have borrowed, Stephen Hall and his paper on *The Great Gatsby* and Elizabeth Katz and her paper on the writings of James Baldwin.

My wife, Lois, has been always an invaluable editor for my writings and increasingly she has become a co-author whose cooperation is indispensable.

Finally, I would like to thank Edwin Seaver whose editing has made the book more readable and coherent.

# Preface

This is a book about the American novel written by an historian. I have ventured across the traditional dividing line between history and literature because our novelists have played a crucial role in shaping the controlling assumptions that I bring to the analysis and writing of history.

The present essay is closely linked to an earlier book, *Historians Against History: The Frontier Thesis and the National Covenant in American Historical Writing Since 1830.* There I argued that a central tradition in American historical writing has been the assumption that the United States, unlike the European nations, has a covenant that makes Americans a chosen people who have escaped from the terror of historical change to live in timeless harmony with nature. From the beginning of the nineteenth century until today, many of our historians have written intricate metaphysical and theological narratives to demonstrate that change throughout the history of the republic is mere appearance and that ultimate reality in America resides in the immutable time of origins in 1776 or 1789.

As a graduate student, at the end of the nineteen forties, my understanding of American history was based on the theories of Frederick Jackson Turner, Charles A. Beard, and Vernon Louis Parrington, three major prophets of the national covenant with nature. But the writings of certain of our literary critics began to plant seeds of doubt in my mind that timeless unity was indeed the reality of the American experience. And my reading in the works of our novelists persuaded me that the reality of American history, like all history, is that of timeful change, timeful because change is always linked to the past and is always leading into the future. It was from the novelists that I learned to identify the frontier hypothesis used by the professional historians not with scientific and neutral objectivity, but with a theology of salvation for the American nation.

Our novelists have led me to believe that the great drama of American intellectual history has been the hope of the European emigrants in coming to the New World: they could there undergo a religious experience of rebirth which would allow them to transcend the tension of the historical communities of the Old World. Our novels have convinced me that this tension is inevitable because the human community must always have roots in the past even as it must have a vision of the future.

I hope to follow this book with one that considers the relationship of eminent American public philosophers like Jefferson and Emerson, James and Dewey, Lippmann and Niebuhr, to the European dream of redemption in the virgin land of America. The conflict between the idea of nature and the idea of civilization, it seems to me, is central to the philosophical concerns of each of these, and the major patterns of their metaphysics and theology are built upon their definition of the ultimate reality of the United States as either a state of nature or a continuation of European civilization.

For me, the central focus of the history of ideas has become the analysis of the way a community defines its place in time, its relationship to the past and to the future. Its historians, its novelists, its poets, artists and musicians, its philosophers, theologians and scientists, are all concerned with this crucial problem of finding or imposing meaning upon the odyssey of the community in time.

Since I am an historian, my first recognition of the attempt by modern Americans to escape the problem of time found expression in the analysis of our historical writings. But it is also possible to suggest that our novels, because they deal with the history of an individual or a group of individuals, have forced their authors always to confront and often to criticize the central myth of our civilization—the transcendence of time.

# Contents

# I

## THE JEREMIAHS

*James Fenimore Cooper*
*Nathaniel Hawthorne*
*Herman Melville*

The novel of eighteenth-century England was concerned with the comedy and tragedy inherent in the revolutionary social mobility which characterized the emergence of a middle class within the traditions of an older and more static class structure. On a scale unprecedented in human history, individuals were free to rise and fall within an existing class hierarchy. The novelist was exploiting the drama of individuals who had suddenly achieved a qualified freedom within a community that had become partially fluid.

The hero or heroine of the rising middle class was infatuated with the idea of the self-made man who could transcend not only the limitations of social institutions and traditions but the weaknesses of human nature itself. The novelist could then choose to emphasize the comedy or the tragedy of the history of the romantic individual who eventually learned of the fixed boundaries which society and innate human failings placed upon these pretensions of omnipotence. The reader, according to his predisposition, would laugh or weep as the protagonist's dreams were ground into the dust of reality by the millstones of social necessity and human foible.

But the American novel, born at the beginning of the nineteenth century, was not to explore these conventional themes of comedy and tragedy within the context of the human condition. In the new American nation the romanticism of the developing bourgeoisie, the myth of the self-made man, came to be accepted as the reality rather than the dream of human existence. It was proclaimed, in the United States of 1830, that every man had transcended the human condition to achieve perfect freedom in harmony with redemptive nature. Ironically, it was the thrust of romantic ideology in Europe which made possible this concept of American exceptionalism.

By 1800, the major intellectual tendencies of western civilization were moving rapidly from the more sober expectations of the Enlightenment to the unbounded aspirations of romanticism. The European romantics had begun to dream of a hero who might transcend the restraints of society and the limitations of human nature to achieve total earthly fulfillment. This exceptional hero was to gain the strength for breaking his personal and social bonds by achieving organic union with nature; he would tap the vast power of the earth mother.

In America, however, where the West stretched to the distant horizon as a great and magnificent expanse of virgin land, it was possible for every man to achieve this romantic vision of the European poets and even to transcend it. Here the common man, the people, would realize the good that English and German poets held out only for heroes and supermen. The soaring faith of the American romantic affirmed the ability of the average citizen to rise above his personal weaknesses and the traditions and institutions of his European ancestors because, in the United States, every individual was in close contact with nature; the West was a limitless national reservoir of spiritual strength.

In the history of America's popular imagination, the precise coming of this heaven on earth has a political date —1828. It is the election of Andrew Jackson that symbolizes the triumph of democracy and the common man. And with this end of colonial political culture comes the end of America's relationship to the European past. The human condition of mankind, it is proclaimed, hitherto always tragic or comic, has given way to an earthly millennium of perfect harmony in the New World Eden. The American democratic citizen is a new Adam. After 1828, there will be no drama in America, there can be no drama where all is the timeless and immutable harmony in which every man has transcended all social and individual limitations. Where all is perfection, there can be nothing novel in the life of any individual. It follows, there is no place for the novelist in this Eden.

The American novelist then, beginning with James Fenimore Cooper, cannot write within the traditional conventions of his European contemporaries. He is precluded by his nation's romantic self-image from being an analyst of social and individual comedy or tragedy. Our novelist must be a metaphysician and theologian. He must always begin with the question: Is it possible that Americans are exempt from the human condition? Is it possible that men in the New World have escaped from the need to live within community, within a framework of institutions and traditions —have escaped even from the need to live within a mortal body, or with a soul that is divided against itself? Can nature indeed redeem man, heal his spiritual divisions, and lift him above the constraints of social class?

Our major novelists, from James Fenimore Cooper to Saul Bellow, are public philosophers and theologians who continually test the national faith in an American Adam living in a New World Eden against their experience with the human situation; they must test the validity of innocence as the American condition. Until the national community ceases to define itself as a congregation of earthly saints living outside of historical culture, our novelists have no choice but to make their heroes philosophers and theologians who contrast their initiation into the realities of America with this ideal.

The first generation of great American novelists—Cooper, Hawthorne, and Melville—lived through the decades when the national faith was reaching triumphant expression in the development of Jacksonian democracy. It is the concept of the American Adam that each of these men makes central in his writing. They deny that America can become a New World Eden, and they reject the heavenly city on earth as a worthwhile or defensible ideal; they refuse to believe in the perfectibility of man.

It has been fashionable to interpret Cooper as a celebrant of the American Adam in his Leatherstocking novels in spite of our knowledge that he vehemently criticized Jacksonian democracy in his political writings. In fact, the Leatherstocking tales are an allegorical attack on the American Adam; they complement rather than contradict Cooper's political objections to the American democratic faith. Professor R. W. B. Lewis sees the figure of the American Adam as a key to understanding the great recurrent themes of our nineteenth-century literature. This is a hero, he writes, who "seems to take his start outside of time . . . his initial habitat is space as spaciousness, as the unbounded, the area of total possibility."* To understand fully Cooper's use of this symbolic figure as Natty Bumppo, we must first contrast it with the American Adam who fills the pages of the greatest apologist of Jacksonian democracy, the historian George Bancroft.

A New Englander, Bancroft extended his Harvard

---

*R. W. B. Lewis, *The American Adam* (Univ. of Chicago, 1955).

training in Germany and then returned to participate as the head of the party of the people in Massachusetts in the revolution which ended the eighteenth century in America. His massive multi-volume history of the United States* is the justification of that revolution, and is explicit in its affirmation that the Jacksonians had destroyed the last vestiges of European culture in the New World. Bancroft held that the democrats of 1830 were only completing a process of purification that had begun during the American Revolution.

It was Washington, he wrote, who was the first great romantic hero struggling to liberate the people from the corrupt limitations of European society, to free them to enjoy the redemptive caress of nature. Washington, for Bancroft, had the strength to destroy history because he was the child of nature. "His culture was altogether his own work, and he was in the strictest sense a self-made man. . . . At sixteen he went into the wilderness as a surveyor, and for three years continued the pursuit, where the forests trained him, in meditative solitude, to freedom and largeness of mind."

But Washington, for Bancroft, did not completely succeed in destroying European influence and establishing the nation firmly as a state of nature with a completely redeemed citizenry. This was not to be, he wrote, until the valley of democracy, the great interior basin of the Mississippi, was settled. There Americans would achieve an organic relationship to the virgin land. There every man would become a child of nature. Led by Andrew Jackson, these reborn people, these natural democrats, would recross the Appalachian Mountains and drive from the east coast all vestiges of European institutions and traditions.

Jackson, like Washington, was an "orphan hero" who in his "infancy sported in the ancient forests, and his mind was nursed to freedom by their influence . . . this child of the woodlands, this representative of forest life in the West,

---

* George Bancroft, *History of the United States* (Little, Brown, 1840).

appeared modestly and firmly on the side of liberty. . . .
Behold, then, the unlettered man of the West, the nursling
of the wilds . . . little versed in books . . . raised by the will
of the people. . . . What policy will he pursue? What wisdom
will he bring with him from the forest?

"The man of the West came as the inspired prophet of
the West: he came as one free from the bonds of hereditary
or established custom . . . it was the office of Jackson to lift
the country out of European forms of legislation, and to
open to it a career resting on American sentiment and
American freedom."

Here, in Bancroft's portraits of Washington and Jackson, these two "orphan heroes" whose only true parent is the
forest, we find the perfect expression of Professor Lewis'
American Adam who "seems to take his start outside of
time."

# 1

We, the children of Jacksonian romanticism, have always
been seduced into believing what we have wanted to
believe—that Leatherstocking is a brother of Bancroft's
Washington and Jackson. But a different reading, one that
begins with *Deerslayer* and concludes with *The Prairie*, reveals Cooper's dedication to the death of the American
Adam by placing him within time. Systematically, he proceeds to destroy Leatherstocking's "initial habitat . . . as
spaciousness." Leatherstocking's "area of total possibility"
becomes more and more constricted until a withered myth
vanishes with the disappearance of the last area of virgin
land. Where Bancroft's histories affirm the fulfillment of the
romantic dream in America, Cooper's novels counter with
an emphatic No!

Bancroft's epic narrative reaches its first great climax
in the French and Indian War. The triumph of nature, he

wrote, was in doubt until this struggle was decided. It was only when Protestant England and Prussia destroyed the influence of Catholic France and Spain in the New World that it became certain that European civilization was not to corrupt American nature. The defeat of the French guaranteed that the West, the valley of democracy, was to retain the redemptive virtue of its virgin state until the American people could establish natural democracy there after the American Revolution. The fulfillment of Jacksonian democracy depended upon the preservation of the West from defilement by European hands in 1760. It was this West which, for Bancroft, was to provide that "space as spaciousness" on which the future of the American Adam as "total possibility" was to depend.

Engaged in critical debate with the Jacksonians, it is not surprising that Cooper begins the life history of Leatherstocking, as Deerslayer, in the opening years of the crucial struggle between England and France for the control of the Mississippi Valley. Professor Lewis has written: "If there was a fictional Adamic hero unambiguously treated—celebrated in his very Adamism—it was the hero of Cooper's *The Deerslayer:* a self-reliant young man who does seem to have sprung from nowhere and whose characteristic pose . . . was the solitary stance in the presence of Nature and God." * Here apparently is the first great literary celebration of the American orphan hero, raised to stalwart manhood by the forest.

But Cooper does not allow his hero to live outside of time and society in "the presence of Nature and God." Deerslayer marches to the discordant harmonies of human warfare unable to enjoy the motionless harmony of eternal nature. Cooper does not place the American Adam within history; he places the myth of the American Adam within history.

The novel begins then with Deerslayer, the orphan

---

*Lewis, *op. cit.*

child of the forest, in the company of Hurry Harry. Clearly, the saintly and innocent Deerslayer is defined as a myth by the flesh and blood presence of Hurry Harry who is the real American Adam—massive, vigorous, handsome, seed of the Eternal Adam. Selfish, vain, and cruel, he lives in the redemptive bosom of nature but he is not redeemed. It is clear that his character will never change.

Pushing on westward to the Glimmerglass, we meet Hutter's daughter, Judith, the American Eve. She too is her father's daughter, not the child of nature. Hutter has fled his past as a pirate but this frontier body of water has not washed away his sinfulness which has been inherited by his beautiful daughter. There is biting irony in Cooper's portrait of Hutter's other daughter, Hetty. Here at last we meet someone as pure and innocent as Deerslayer himself. But her goodness comes neither from the influence of the frontier or from her own choice. She transcends the human condition because she is insane.

Cooper begins by telling us that the dream held by the American public, this dream that European character will be redeemed by virgin land, can never be fulfilled. Americans will remain forever the children of their European parents. There will never be an American Adam. It is the old, the Eternal Adam and Eve who will populate the frontier. But Cooper is not content to argue the impossibility of the dream. He reveals the irony inherent in the Jacksonian's faith that the birth of the American Adam can separate the New World from the Old.

With the harsh logic of a Jeremiah, he asks his readers to consider the context in which Deerslayer appears. It is the time of the struggle between England and France for the West. Is there any alternative then but to define Deerslayer as the projection of the English imagination? Deerslayer is the embodiment of an English myth. It is Englishmen who believe that they can achieve redemption by escaping from the cultural complexity of the past to the primitive purity of nature. How paradoxical, that Americans should use an English myth to define their independence from England!

Cooper explores the role of this myth in the English imagination. Englishmen have dreamed of escape from the evil in their own hearts by making their exodus into the promised land beyond the mountains. As they march toward the West, they follow their dream in the symbolic figure of Deerslayer, who represents the innocence they hope to achieve. When they reach the borders of Eden, however, they find their way barred by the French and Indians. Suddenly, the frontier changes from a vision of peace into the reality of a battleground. Englishmen are human; they are not earthly saints. They will fight and kill their human brothers to achieve their goal of harmony. In the name of innocence, they will prove their mortality, and so their visionary leader must change from a Deerslayer, living in harmony with nature, into a warrior, Hawkeye, who will defeat their enemies and clear the path into the Eden of the continental interior. This is the drama of the novel—Deerslayer's loss of innocence—because the myth must change to serve the interests of the culture which created it. Deerslayer is a child of history, not of nature. He and the myth he represents have a history; he must change through time. Ultimately he, too, must die.

Desperately, Deerslayer attempts to preserve his neutrality in the struggle between the English and their enemies, to remain as his English fathers envisioned him: the child of nature, symbol of peace and harmony. Ultimately, however, he has no choice but to fight to protect the Anglo-Americans against their enemies.

The dramatic turning point in the novel is reached when Deerslayer kills a man for the first time, in defense of the Hutter family. He has wished to avoid conflict but he has to keep the canoe, the key to the safety of the family on the lake, out of the hands of the attacking Indians. This act of social commitment forces him to kill the Indian who threatens to capture the canoe. It is his dying victim who tells him he has lost his innocence. Deerslayer, he says, "That good name for boy—poor name for warrior . . . eye sartain—finger lightning—aim, death—great warrior soon. No Deerslayer—Hawkeye—Hawkeye—Hawkeye."

The man and the myth have lost their innocence. The war of conquest is on and the myth as man will become the strong right arm of his parent culture.

We meet Leatherstocking next in *The Last of the Mohicans*. He is a soldier of the king. The Deerslayer, who could bring himself to kill a man only with the greatest reluctance, is now Hawkeye, efficient, methodical, terrible killer of Indians. At the opening of the novel when Major Heyward brings an Indian scout into camp, Hawkeye warns against the Indian.

" 'Think you so?' said Heyward. 'I confess I have not been without my own suspicions.' "

" 'I knew he was one of the cheats as soon as I laid eyes on him!' returned the scout. 'This thief is leaning against the foot of the sugar sapling that you can see over them bushes; his right leg is in line with the bark of the tree, and . . . I can take him from where I stand between the ankle and the knee.' "

" 'It will not do' [said Heyward]. 'He may be innocent, and I dislike the act.' "

Hawkeye is the cold-blooded frontier fighter who will shoot first and ask questions later. It is the English professional soldier who supplies the restraint and humanity.

*The Last of the Mohicans* demonstrates the continued destruction of the myth by the demands of history. The first novel dramatized Deerslayer's loss of innocence; its sequel deals with the death of the myth as it finds symbolic expression in the noble savage. Chingachgook, the Indian as myth, like Deerslayer, has been forced to fight for the English culture which has created him. We met Chingachgook in

*The Deerslayer* as the only true friend of the American Adam. Indeed, he was more than a friend, he was a brother. In the English millennial dream, the lion would lie down with the lamb in the American Eden. In the mythical West that has sprung from the imagination of these Europeans, the American as natural man can live in harmony with his brother, the Indian as natural man. Yet Chingachgook had to step out of the harmony of nature into the disharmony of history. His son, Uncas, now carries the mythical mantle of innocence which his father has surrendered in joining Hawkeye as a hardened soldier. Uncas and the English girl, Cora, fall in love. If the myth of the American Adam, stripped of the burden of history and standing in that unbounded space which offers boundless possibilities, obtained as reality, then there should be no barrier to the marriage of these two children of nature. But Cooper does present a barrier—the reality of history.

Englishmen are not the children of nature; they are conquerors who will impose their culture on the continent. Nor are the Indians; they are the defenders of their own culture, of their own way of life. When the English will have defeated the French, then the only barrier between them and the West will be the Indian. And when the Indian is seen as the last barrier to the conquest and exploitation of the frontier, white men will no longer be able to believe in the myth of the noble savage. It is only right, therefore, that Uncas, the last of the Mohicans, the last of the noble savages, should die with the defeat of the French, as it is right that he should be killed by Magua. Magua is an Indian of history; he hates the white man for destroying the Indian culture. When he desires Cora, he does so like an Indian; he wants her as an Indian squaw, as the subservient, obedient female of the Indian way of life. Dramatically Cooper reveals the way in which Anglo-American culture will define the Indian after the French and Indian War. The Indian will be Magua, who will fling his curses and his

tomahawk at the white who crosses the mountains into the
Garden. After 1760, the Indian can only be defined as the
barbaric opponent of the spread of Anglo-American civilization westward.

The defeat of France has opened the Ohio and Mississippi valleys to Anglo-American culture. Continuing to place
the Adamic myth within the development of history, Cooper
now presents Leatherstocking as the Pathfinder who will
lead the Europeans into the Garden. According to the Americans of 1830, this area of the Midwest presented a different
kind of nature than that of the east coast. For Cooper's contemporaries, European culture had been able to make a
beachhead along the Atlantic. The virgin land of the coastal
colonies had not been able to redeem Europeans and to
make them into that new man, the innocent American. But
for the Jacksonians, when settlers went across the Appala-
cian Mountains, geography destroyed their heritage of
European civilization and freed them from history to live
in harmony with nature.

In *The Pathfinder*, the hero tries to escape from the
Anglo-American culture which has robbed him of his freedom. Pathfinder dreams of giving up his life as a soldier to
return to innocence. But the myth is still being defined by
history. It is here in the Mississippi Valley, according to
prophecy, that people were to live in harmony in a new kind
of society, a natural society without the complexities and
weaknesses of civilization. Such a society demands the union
of Adam with an Eve in domesticity, surrounded by descendants.

Pathfinder, who is now identified as Adam by Cooper, is
willing to accept this responsibility and marry and become
the archetypical father for a uniquely natural community.
But the people he has led into the new West are human
beings and not saints; they are committed to historical
society. There is no mythical Eve to complement the willing
Adam. Pathfinder falls in love with Mabel but Mabel will

not, indeed she cannot, give up civilization to marry the frontiersman. It is Pathfinder himself who tells the reader that the match should not take place because he recognizes that he is not like other human beings, that he is a species apart. When Mabel finally says, "Pathfinder—dear Pathfinder, understand me . . . a match like that would be unwise—unnatural, perhaps." He agrees: "Yes, unnat'ral—agin natur'."

Cooper obviously hopes that he is driving home a moral to the American people. He has Pathfinder cry out, "What creature is a mortal man! Never satisfied with his own gifts, but forever craving that which Providence denies!" The American people have longed to escape history and live with nature like the Pathfinder, but nature is no substitute for what God has given man: the possibility of love and family and civilization. The utter loneliness of Pathfinder, his longing for the society in which he can never dwell, is given beautiful expression in his dream where he tries to exchange nature for human companionship: "I imagined I had a cabin in a grove of sugar maples, and at the root of every tree was a Mabel Dunham, while the birds sang ballads, instead of the notes that natur' gave."

Certainly the moral of this novel is that Americans need humility, that they need to accept their humanity and frailty. Cooper wanted to teach them that they could never escape from history.

The next novel in the life cycle of Leatherstocking, *The Pioneers*, is an extended elaboration of this point that Americans can never escape their historical past. With the establishment of an independent nation, free from political connection with the British Empire, it was possible to believe that a new kind of civilization, one without historical roots, had been established in the New World.

Deerslayer was the mythical embodiment of the philosophy which described Europe in terms of historical time and America in terms of physical space. But, Cooper argued, how can Americans justify their cultural independence from England on the strength of a myth that is English in origin? The dramatic role of Leatherstocking in *The Pioneers,* therefore, is to unite American and English culture and Cooper reminds his readers that Leatherstocking, the man as myth, is loyal to that civilization which gave him his identity.

Approaching Cooper from the traditional viewpoint that he is celebrating, not criticizing, the myth of virgin land, Henry Nash Smith has noted an element of ambiguity in *The Pioneers.** Cooper, he declares, is presenting a case in favor of civilization when he has Judge Temple speak philosophically to his daughter who has come to the defense of Leatherstocking, guilty of hunting out of season. "Thou hast reason, Bess, and much of it too, but thy heart lies too near thy head. . . . Say what thou wilt to the poor old man; give scope to the feelings of thy warm heart; but try to remember, Elizabeth, that the laws alone remove us from the condition of the savage; that he has been criminal, and that his judge was thy father."

Professor Smith interprets the drama of the novel as the ambiguity between Cooper's commitment to the values of nature symbolized by Leatherstocking and the values of civilization symbolized by Judge Temple. But actually the drama revolves around the reconciliation of the American, Judge Temple, and the Englishman, Major Effingham, a reconciliation which reaches fulfillment in the marriage of the Major's grandson, Oliver Effingham, and Elizabeth Temple.

There is no doubt in Cooper's mind that the values of Judge Temple are superior to those of Leatherstocking. Indeed, the old man is presented as a decrepit myth which survives only through the indulgence of the Judge.

If Leatherstocking as Pathfinder fails to become the archetype of the pioneers, Judge Temple is represented as

---

*Henry Nash Smith, *Virgin Land* (Harvard, 1950).

succeeding. Leatherstocking symbolized the myth which promised that the American pioneers would be Adams and Eves who might step out of time to live with nature's unbounded spaciousness. Now in place of the utopian settlement which Pathfinder could not establish is the community which Judge Temple has built. The Judge is a man of civilization who is bringing complex culture, an historical heritage, to the frontier. He is the man of law because the men and women who came west to live in his community are frail and imperfect human beings who need the law to control their evil and their selfishness. Nature cannot redeem them; indeed these people would quickly destroy nature if the law did not restrain them and in turn give protection to nature.

Judge Temple and Leatherstocking debate this issue. Natty Bumppo, still the embodiment of the myth, argues that man can live in harmony with nature only if he can approach it in a completely free and spontaneous way without the interference of law. Judge Temple makes the counter-argument that given human nature which is always self-seeking and avaricious, men will quickly ravage nature if it is not protected by law. For Cooper, society on the frontier is like all societies, self-destructive unless restrained and governed by enlightened and disinterested men who uphold the law.

Understanding that Leatherstocking represents an ideal which, although erroneous, has dignity, Judge Temple tolerates and even protects the aging myth. It is not the Judge's upholding of the law which ultimately drives Natty Bumppo out of the community, rather it is the lawless mob which has no respect for Leatherstocking's need for privacy and isolation. It is as if the people must mock and harry the fading myth which had failed to redeem them. Indeed, the lingering presence of Leatherstocking with his superior virtue and purity infuriates the people who cannot rise to his level of behavior.

But the most important role of Leatherstocking in *The Pioneers* is to facilitate the reconciliation of Judge Temple and Major Effingham, that is, the reconciliation of American and English culture, the understanding of Americans for their historical tradition.

Cooper does not trust his contemporaries to understand the symbolism of reunion and continuity with the past. He becomes even more explicit about the role of Natty Bumppo in bringing together American and British culture. Did the readers understand that Deerslayer had become a soldier of the king, and that the myth had been used by Englishmen to steel the nerve and arms of their invading force? Now even as Major Effingham, the last direct symbol of English culture, lies dying in America, so Leatherstocking, who has served the English conquerors so well, has lost his vitality and is withering away. His final constructive achievement is to keep his commander alive until his rightful claim to be a part of the American frontier is recognized. And Cooper does not merely suggest the commander and follower relationship, he spells it out in literal form, graven in the granite of Major Effingham's tombstone for all future Americans to see as the evidence of the relationship of the myth to the English heritage.

At the end of the novel Leatherstocking leaves for the unsettled frontier. On his first trip to the area of virgin land as the Pathfinder, he had turned back because he could not serve as the father of settlement. The myth had failed to fulfill itself; it could not separate itself from the civilization which had brought it into existence, and so Leatherstocking returned to the real father of settlement, Judge Temple. Here he could play the constructive role of illuminating the relationship of American and English society. If the myth could not separate itself from historical culture, it could clarify its relationship to that history and demonstrate that it was a tradition which united America to the past. Having revealed, however, that America was to be defined in terms of history and time and not in terms of unbounded space, what future and function did the myth now have?

When Leatherstocking sets out for the unsettled areas of the West as an old and withered figure in the 1790's, he could not go hoping for fulfillment. That hope had been crushed a generation before in *The Pathfinder*. Leatherstocking, alone, might still find harmony with nature but he could not found a new society. And any such harmony must be temporary because Leatherstocking was a prisoner of time. Human settlement constantly overran the virgin land which had given him strength; as the area of unspoiled nature shrank, he in turn withered away. But as long as there was an unsettled area, Americans would continue to believe in the myth that they might escape history to live with nature. Leatherstocking could not perish as long as there was a last frontier.

It is with sadness and resignation that the old man sets out for the West to spend his few remaining days. He knows that these days are numbered because inevitably settlers will come to the virgin land, and when there will be no more land without human habitation, there will be no more myth. The stage is carefully set for the final novel of the series, *The Prairie*.

The myth, for Cooper, must end with settlement because the settlers are human; they will carry disharmony engraved indelibly in their hearts. They will have all the human weakness that the first frontier Adam and Eve, Hurry Harry and Judith, had demonstrated in *The Deerslayer*. It is difficult to visualize how Cooper could have provided greater dramatic emphasis to this point than by painting the picture of the Ishmael Bush family, which is the first invader of Leatherstocking's last refuge. Here is vulgarity and brutality in its most exaggerated form.

Cooper's literary art reaches its highest level when he brings the Bush family and Leatherstocking to their first confrontation, which has the dramatic implication of

Leatherstocking's doom and the death of the myth. Bursting with crude vitality, the Bush family is pushing westward toward their evening camp when suddenly out of the setting sun there grew a fantastic apparition: "The sun had fallen below the crest of the nearest wave of the prairie, leaving the usual rich and glowing train as its track. In the center of this flood of fiery light, a human form appeared, drawn against the gilded background as distinctly, and seemingly as palpable, as though it would come within the grasp of any extended hand. The figure was colossal; the attitude musing and melancholy, and the situation directly in the route of the travellers. But, imbedded, as it was, in its setting of garish light, it was impossible to distinguish its just proportions or true character."

Brilliantly, Cooper has captured the situation of the myth. Only in the setting sun of the western prairie does Leatherstocking promise to be larger than life. And when the family comes to see the reality as the sun sets and shadows creep across the prairie, all they find is a withered, almost mummified, old man.

The myth has come to the final frontier to accept its fate. It is as if Leatherstocking, through his human suffering in the death of Major Effingham, has achieved a bond of understanding and sympathy with mankind that makes him a spokesman for the superiority of civilization to nature. A myth that embodies nature, he cannot choose to live in civilization. But he can warn those who would attempt to flee from civilization to turn back to accept their human responsibility. He can demonstrate, in the withering of his own body, the fallacy of the American belief in the unrestricted possibilities for men in the unbounded spaciousness of nature. There is no escape from the cycle of life and death, no escape from the ravages of time.

The action of this final novel takes place during Jefferson's administration. The President had dispatched Lewis and Clarke to explore the vast territories acquired in the Louisiana Purchase. The nation has hopes that this tremendous area will guarantee redemptive contact with nature for generations to come. But Cooper has placed the aging Leatherstocking on this new land, which the author describes as a dry and almost lifeless desert, the perfect physical complement of the desiccated hunter.

And Leatherstocking, who in *The Pioneers* still argued against Judge Temple's advocacy of conservation, of the use of law to preserve nature, now thinks back to the irresponsible rape of the virgin land:

"What the world of America is coming to, and where the machinations and inventions of its people are to have an end, the Lord, He only knows. . . . How much has the beauty of the wilderness been deformed in two short lives. . . . I often think the Lord has placed this barren belt of prairies behind the States, to warn men to what their folly may yet bring the land."

Leatherstocking now realizes that harmony, whatever harmony exists, comes not spontaneously from nature. It comes painfully from human effort; it is imposed by human law. "The law—'tis bad to have it, but, I sometimes think, it is worse to be entirely without it . . . yes—yes, the law is needed."

To dramatize this point, Cooper returns to the first settlers of this last frontier. The family of Ishmael Bush, coarse, disharmonious, evil, has come to the West to escape the law. As with Hurry Harry and Judith, as with all settlers, they will not be spontaneously redeemed by nature; they will not have a rebirth, will not become innocent. But Ishmael Bush does grow in moral stature. Gradually, he comes to accept the moral implications of his role as head of this first family. He is the head of a new society, and that society cannot exist without human justice and human law. Ishmael Bush begins to be transformed when he accepts the necessity of punishing the murderer who is part of his family. Even in the middle of an unsettled desert, man achieves dignity only through the law.

As the last days of Leatherstocking draw near, Lt. Duncan Uncas Middleton, a representative of the eastern aristocracy, makes his appearance. The last link between the fading myth and its parent culture, he will make it possible for Leatherstocking to perish in peace, secure in the knowledge that his memory will be honored.

"I am without kith or kin in the whole wide world," says Leatherstocking. "When I am gone, there will be an end of my race." The myth could not find embodiment in society and now, with the end of the frontier, it must disappear.

But the myth would find afterlife among the eastern aristocracy; tradition within an historical society does not die. The ancient hunter is brought to tears of happiness as Lt. Middleton tells how his grandfather, Major Middleton of the British Army, taught his children to revere the memory of the noble savage, as represented by Uncas, and the frontiersman, Hawkeye. Our grandfather, says Duncan, taught us that " 'Unlike most of those who live a border life, he Leatherstocking, united the better, instead of the worst, qualities. . . . He was a man endowed with choicest and perhaps rarest gifts of nature; that of distinguishing good from evil. His virtues were those of simplicity. . . . In short, he was a noble shoot from the stock of human nature, which never could attain its proper elevation and importance, for no other reason than because it grew in the forest; such, old hunter, were the very words of my grandfather . . . there are already three among us who have also names derived from that scout.'

" 'A name, did you say?' exclaims the old man, 'what, the name of the solitary, unl'arned hunter? Do the great, the rich, and the honored, and what is better still, the just, do they bear his very, actual name?' "

Assured that his memory will be preserved in living tradition, he can die happy. Here is the final evidence that Cooper did not intend his hero to exist outside of time. Leatherstocking is happy because he will be embedded in time forever, his name will be passed from one generation to another.

As befitting a myth of nature, he does not die as a man. The rituals of Christian civilization have no meaning in his last hours. The spirit of the myth will leave its earthly abode to follow the setting sun westward forever:

"The trapper was placed on a rude seat, which had been made, with studied care, to support his frame in an upright and easy attitude. . . . His body was placed so as to let the light of the setting sun fall full upon the solemn features. . . . The trapper had remained nearly motionless for an hour. His eyes alone had occasionally opened and shut. When opened, his gaze seemed fastened on the clouds which hung around the western horizon. . . . Suddenly . . . Middleton felt the hand which he held grasp his own with incredible power, and the old man, supported on either side by his friends, rose upright to his feet. For a moment, he looked about him . . . and then . . he pronounced the word —'Here!' "

For Cooper, it was here on the great plains, during Jefferson's administration, that the myth of the frontier perished; the last unknown territories had been penetrated by human beings who, by their very presence, destroyed the mysterious potential of the virgin land. "Space as spaciousness, as the unbounded, the area of total possibility," no longer existed.

From the outset, when Deerslayer was forced to participate in the disharmony of history, Cooper had prepared for this moment. The five Leatherstocking novels are a sustained argument against the autonomous existence of an American Adam. Inexorably, Cooper has forced the myth to live within the historical rhythm of the Anglo-American culture which had created it. The history of Leatherstocking parallels the history of his society from 1740 to 1800.

D. H. Lawrence contended that "The Leatherstocking novels . . . go backwards from old age to golden youth. That is the true myth of America. She starts old, old, wrinkled and writhing in an old skin. And there is a gradual sloughing off of the old skin, towards a new youth. It is the myth of America."* It is, indeed, the myth of America, the myth that Cooper set out to destroy by tracing its history from the freshness of youth to its demise, old and wrinkled, on the last frontier.

## 2

Cooper had explored the myth of the American Adam and related it to the drive of Anglo-American culture in the second half of the eighteenth century to conquer the trans-Appalachian West. He described Leatherstocking as a projection of the English imagination upon the American landscape and believed that, logically, this imagination would cease to operate with the settlement of the last area of virgin land. He was asking his Jacksonian contemporaries to surrender their faith in a myth which had exhausted its vitality. Cooper was still trying to disestablish the myth in the 1840's, long after the death of Natty Bumppo. Did this idea of American uniqueness and innocence have such deep roots that it could transcend the boundaries of the Jeffersonian covenant with nature?

For Nathaniel Hawthorne, descendant of New England Puritans, the answer was yes. He saw that the myth of the American Adam had existed before 1740 and would survive the end of the frontier; its roots were in that religious faith called Puritanism. The belief in the possibility

---

* D. H. Lawrence, *Studies in Classic American Literature* (Viking, 1964).

of European rebirth and regeneration in the New World was the motivating vision which had led the saving remnant from England to Massachusetts; the American Adam was the theological creation of the English thinkers of 1600 who supposed that it was possible to flee from the sinfulness of old England to the innocence of New England.

But Hawthorne did not believe in the saving remnant; the human condition was the inescapable context of man's experience on this earth. Always man had sinned and in his sinfulness created an historical community as his necessary environment. Looking back at his Puritan ancestors, Hawthorne found no earthly saints, only mortal men who deluded themselves that they were. In denying their sinfulness, these Puritans had committed the unforgivable sin of denying their own humanity. They had refused to acknowledge their historical parents, their lineage to the Eternal Adam, and created instead that abstract creature without roots and, therefore, without the quality of mercy —the American Adam.

As Hawthorne witnessed the enthusiasm of the Jacksonians and their philosophical cousins, the Transcendentalists, for the achievement of an American Eden, he must have been struck by this strange historical parallel in which romantic American democrats viewed themselves as latter-day saints breathing new life into the moribund dream of 1630. Two centuries had passed, and now this great reform movement of the 1830's once again proclaimed Americans to be a saving remnant destined to light a beacon on a hill for all mankind to follow in their progress out of history and evil upward toward nature and purity.

Like Cooper, Hawthorne perceived the central irony in this drama: he saw the logical impossibility of Americans defining their independence from Europe in terms of a theological myth made in Europe. But he was to go beyond Cooper's description of the absurdity of judging commonsense experience by the standards of European metaphysics.

He asked his readers to discover the central truth about themselves—that they were accommodating their lives to a transcendent script written by European theoreticians who hated the historical experience of mankind. What is revealed in Hawthorne's masterpiece, *The Scarlet Letter,* is the human tragedy that must follow any attempt of Americans to live in alienation from the rest of the human race.

His brief introductory chapter, "The Prison," establishes the philosophical and theological context within which he is to judge the Puritan experiment. "The Founders of a new colony, whatever Utopia of human virtue and happiness they might originally project, have invariably recognized it among their earliest practical necessities to allot a portion of the virgin soil as a cemetery, and another portion as the site of a prison." This contradiction between the ideal and the real was, for Hawthorne, the beginning of the peculiar American tragedy he was about to relate. European men had here in Massachusetts established a human society as mortal and fallible as themselves. Nevertheless, they had proclaimed themselves as earthly saints who had withdrawn from their sinful brothers in Europe to establish a Kingdom of God in the New World. The great expectation of these Puritans was that none of their elect membership would sin; they refused to accept weakness as the necessary human condition in this new land where rebirth promised the possibility of Adamic innocence.

And so the tragedy begins to unfold. Gathered in the market place to watch the judgment of an inmate of the prison are the Puritan women who had fed on "the beef and ale of their native land, with a moral diet not a whit more refined." Human beings, not saints, they become vicious hypocrites as they heap criticism on the prisoner with whose weakness they refuse to identify.

Who is this prisoner? What wrong has she committed? Near the darkness of the prison, grows the wild rose with its "delicate gems" to show that, unlike the Puritans, "the deep heart of Nature could pity and be kind." And then out of the gloomy shadows of the prison steps Hester Prynne with all the radiance and beauty of the wild rose. Symbolizing the color, the vivacity she brings to the world is the scarlet letter, the "A," which adorns her breast. Hester's sin is that she has borne an illegitimate child; she must wear this letter to signify that she is an adulteress.

The Puritans believe that they are banning a sinner from their midst, but it is they who are cut off, who have become evil in disassociating themselves from her. Hester has escaped the greater sinfulness of the Puritan community, which is pride. The scarlet letter unites her with the Eternal Adam and "the sinful brotherhood of mankind." And "God, as a direct consequence of the sin which man thus punished, had given her a lovely child . . . to connect her parent forever with the race and descent of mortals, and to be finally a blessed soul in heaven."

Hester Prynne was the English child of the medieval past, taken from a dying aristocracy by "a figure of the study and the cloister." This man of abstract ideals, unable to impose his philosophy of timeless perfection on the historical community of England, had fled with his prize to Holland, lest she be reabsorbed into the corrupt society of the mother country. But although he was husband to Hester, he was sterile, which is the way of immutable perfection: there was no place in his faith for life, for growth and change. Ultimately he had sent Hester to Massachusetts where, in the New World Eden, isolated from the mortal world of Europe, human beings could transcend their nature and live contentedly by his abstract principles of lifeless impotency. Surely this philosopher-theologian was meant by Hawthorne to represent the archetypical Puritan.

As Hester looks out upon the crowd which had gathered to scorn her, she sees the evil countenance of her husband,

Roger Chillingworth. He had come to the New World to witness the successful expression of his theology in the perfect community of Puritan saints; instead he finds that his ideal has been shattered. Hester has not remained barren. Life with its timeful imperfection has appeared in Eden. One of the Puritan saints has fathered her child, thereby blasting Chillingworth's dream of perfection. It is against this traitor to Puritan theology that he pledges his vengeance.

Chillingworth is the true American who, like Leatherstocking, seems "to have sprung from nowhere and whose characteristic pose . . . was the solitary stance in the presence of nature and God." Although he has come into this human and basically European community by way of the American forest, communion with nature has not brought him closer to God. Indeed, he seems to have entered into a compact with the devil, since he has chosen "to withdraw his name from the roll of mankind." Now this man of maniacal dedication to abstractions will masquerade as a physician until he can unmask the father of Hester's child, Pearl.

With dramatic emphasis, Hawthorne introduces us to the man for whom Chillingworth is searching, the minister Arthur Dimmesdale, the symbolic son upon whom the burden of conflict with the Puritan father has fallen. Dimmesdale must struggle between loyalty to Chillingworth's theology of sterile perfection and his experience that the life of man is fruitful imperfection. The dramatic question that grips us for the rest of the novel is whether Dimmesdale will acknowledge his humanity by admitting that it is his seed which has brought forth Pearl from Hester's body. Will the son of the American Adam acknowledge that he is in fact the son of the Eternal Adam?

Dimmesdale is the well-intentioned Puritan who would impose the order of metaphysics and theology on the disorderly experience of life, but is unable to renounce the human condition. Such is his dedication that he cannot conceive of being able to minister to his people if he is an acknowledged sinner. This is the irony that Hawthorne makes central to his tale. Dimmesdale is the most beloved minister in the community precisely because he admits inwardly that he is a sinner. He has learned that man's spirit is as fallible and mortal as his body and his greatest need, therefore, is for love and pity. It was his sin, "this very burden . . . that gave him sympathies so intimate with the sinful brotherhood of mankind, so that his heart vibrated in unison with theirs, and received their pain unto itself."

If Dimmesdale has become the witness of the Eternal Adam in the new world, Hester is his Eve. When she first stands before the magistrates he pleads with her to divulge the name of her seducer—for the good of the father, who has not the strength to save himself from the continuing sin of concealment. He himself feels the impulse to confess, but only from his overwhelming sense of guilt defined by Chillingworth's standards. He has not yet learned that his redemption depends upon his acceptance of the responsibility of fatherhood. But when, several years later, Hester is brought before Governor Bellingham by those who want Pearl taken away from her mother, we see that a change is taking place in him.

Hester has been able to survive among the Puritans because, despite Chillingworth, they continue to live by many of the traditional values of the English historical community. They purchase her beautiful embroidery, the same kind they see daily in the magnificent "A" upon her breast. The exquisite artistry of her needle fills their need to escape the depressing drabness of their lives. Indeed, it is the leaders who are her best customers and the most tolerant. Governor Bellingham's house is decorated with all the richness of English precedent for a political and social leader; even the most important elder, Reverend Wilson, continues to uphold the principles of diversity and tolerance which he had learned in the English universities. When complaint against Hester is brought to them, they want to help this woman whom they secretly admire.

The complaint is that Pearl is being raised without discipline. And it is true that Hester, in spite of every effort, has not been able to make her child amenable to rules. There is also the complaint that she dresses Pearl outside of the norms of the community; Hester has defiantly clothed her in brightness and in beauty. It is necessary for Hawthorne's allegory that this child, like her mother, stand apart in radiance from the others, just as it is important symbolically that Hester is unable to teach Pearl the ways of morality. We mortals need the restraint of law as well as the warmth of love, and since Hester is without law, she cannot provide it for her daughter. Until Dimmesdale accepts his responsibility as a father, he cannot give his wife and child the law that will make them a part of the community and fulfill their humanity.

He does, however, provide the argument that salves the conscience of Governor Bellingham and Reverend Wilson, so that they can justify Hester's continued custody of her daughter. "God gave her this child," he declares. "Therefore it is good for this poor, sinful woman that she hath an infant immortality, a being capable of eternal joy or sorrow, confided to her care—to be trained up by her to righteousness —to remind her, at every moment, of her fall, but yet to teach her, as it were by the Creator's sacred pledge, that, if she brings the child to heaven, the child also will bring the parent thither." And he cries out how much more fortunate the mother is than the father since she has this burden of responsibility that can lead to her salvation. Dimmesdale has accepted the un-Puritanical doctrine of the forgiveness of sins.

But while Governor Bellingham and Reverend Wilson, like Dimmesdale, give Hester and Pearl their love, they will not admit that these outcasts need to be accepted in the community before they are made whole. And this, of course, is impossible until it is acknowledged that ours is a human and not a saintly society. These men still live under the burden of Chillingworth's theology.

When Dimmesdale becomes ill from the secret burden of guilt he carries locked within himself, his parishioners persuade him to allow the alleged physician, Roger Chillingworth, to share his bachelor's quarters, so that the doctor will have every opportunity to diagnose the mysterious ailment which is causing their beloved minister to waste away. But Chillingworth has already identified Dimmesdale as the object of his vengeance. He has seen him one night on the scaffold where the guilt-tormented minister had come to confess his sin to the empty air. There by chance Dimmesdale was joined by Hester and Pearl and had taken them by hand as his wife and child.

"The moment he did so, there came what seemed a tumultuous rush of new life, other life than his own, pouring like a torrent into his heart, and hurrying through all his veins, as if the mother and the child were communicating their vital warmth to his half-torpid system." But when Pearl asks him, "Wil't thou stand here with mother and me tomorrow noontide?" he answers sadly that he cannot so act until "the great judgment day."

By failing to reveal the true identity of Chillingworth, Hester has put into his power the man she loves. Now, intercepting Dimmesdale in the forest, she tells him who Chillingworth is, and proposes that they flee to Europe to begin a new life. As she tears the scarlet letter from her breast, "all at once, with a sudden smile of heaven, forth burst the sunshine, pouring a very flood into the obscure forest, gladdening each green leaf . . . Such was the sympathy of Nature—that wild, heathen Nature of the forest, never subjugated by human law nor illumined by higher truth—with the bliss of these two spirits." But Hawthorne has constantly associated Chillingworth with the forest, and his theology of saintly perfection with the context of American nature. When Hester encourages Dimmesdale to see in nature the possibility of escape from Chillingworth she is, of course, only placing her beloved even more in the power of the wicked physician.

Nature, for Hawthorne, can sustain the body but not the spirit. The human spirit can thrive only in a society compounded of love and responsibility, love and law. Therefore Pearl, for whom the forest is "the playmate of the lonely infant," is incomplete in her wildness because she has no father to teach her that she has a responsible relationship to "the sinful brotherhood of mankind." And wild she must remain until she experiences "a grief that should deeply touch her, and thus humanize her and make her capable of sympathy."

When Pearl joins Hester and Dimmesdale in the forest and sees that her mother has cast off the scarlet letter, she insists that Hester replace the "A" on her bosom. "Now thou art my mother indeed," she says. And when Hester asks her to give the minister her love, she asks: "Doth he love us? Will he go back with us, hand in hand, we three together into the town?" When she receives a negative reply, she washes away his kiss with the water of the brook.

Dimmesdale longs for a new life, when innocence will again be his, but his thought of fleeing from the responsibility of fatherhood—and thus his responsibility for the continuity of the human community—brings him to the brink of Chillingworth's sin. He feels that he is being tempted by the devil, that unless he remains in the community and fully accepts his responsibility, he will indeed be doomed to serve Satan. And thus realizing, he experiences a true rebirth, and emerges from the forest "with a knowledge of hidden mysteries, which the simplicity of the former never could have reached."

When he delivers his serman the next day, Dimmesdale speaks not about the timeless perfection of the present but about the love and beauty that will fill a timeless future. And because the fulfillment of his prophecy depends upon his own action, he walks directly from the church to the scaffold and there, surrounded by his people, he calls upon Hester and Pearl to join him, even as Chillingworth declares: "Hadst thou sought the whole earth over . . . there was no place so secret,—no high place nor lowly place, where thou couldst have escaped me,—save on this scaffold."

Dimmesdale tears open his shirt and reveals to the world the scarlet letter indelibly stamped over his heart. He has transcended the temptation of Hester's cry to "Begin all anew! . . . Whither leads yonder forest-track? . . . Deeper it goes, and deeper, into the wilderness. . . . There thou art free!" He has recognized that in the forest one is only free to choose, like Roger Chillingworth, "to withdraw his name from the roll of mankind"; that his only choice would be to live with the sterile companionship of Chillingworth. Abandoning the sterility of innocence, he calls for his daughter, " 'My little Pearl . . . dear little Pearl, wilt thou kiss me now? Thou wouldst not yonder in the forest! But now thou wilt?' Pearl kissed his lips. A spell was broken. The great scene of grief, in which the wild infant bore a part, had developed all her sympathies; and as her tears fell upon her father's cheek, they were the pledge that she would grow up amid human joy and sorrow, nor forever do battle with the world, but be a woman in it."

What final meaning did Hawthorne hope Americans would learn from this allegory? After a novel of complex and sophisticated symbolism, he enters directly into the conclusion to speak clearly in his own voice. There were, he writes, many respectable witnesses who denied that the minister had revealed himself as the father of Pearl or the bearer of the scarlet letter. But, he adds, "Without disputing a truth so momentous, we must be allowed to consider this version of Mr. Dimmesdale's story as only an instance of that stubborn fidelity with which a man's friends—and especially a clergyman's—will sometimes uphold his character, when proofs, clear as the mid-day sunshine on the scarlet letter, establish him a false and sin-stained creature of the dust.

"Among many morals which press upon us from the poor minister's miserable experience, we put only this into a sentence: 'Be true! Be true! Be true! Show freely to the world, if not your worst, yet some trait whereby the worst may be inferred!' "

The Jacksonians dismissed Hawthorne's novel as a romance which had no practical meaning for a people committed to the worship of common-sense experience. The same public which had twisted Cooper's intention chose to ignore Hawthorne's. Secure in his Garden, the American Adam, having achieved perfection, felt he needed no philosophical or theological advice.

# 3

Like Cooper and Hawthorne, Herman Melville had cultural roots in the colonial past. But he was to a greater extent swept up by the popular current of utopianism which had captured the new nation in the opening decades of the nineteenth century. For the young Melville, the myth of virgin land was a reality: "We are the heirs of all time, and with all nations we divide our inheritance," he declared, anticipating Whitman. "On this Western Hemisphere all tribes and peoples are forming into one federated whole; and there is a future which shall see the estranged children of Adam restored as to the old hearthstone in Eden. . . . The Seed is sown, and the harvest must come." *

The youthful Melville believed in the myth of the noble savage at the moment the mature Cooper was at-

---

*Herman Melville, *Redburn: His First Voyage* (Doubleday: Anchor, 1957).

tempting to destroy it. He believed that men should step out of history into nature, out of disharmony into harmony, out of evil into perfection. But he soon came to doubt the American fulfillment of this dream and went to sea to restore his faith in the regenerative force of nature. Away from an already over-civilized America, he sailed to find the living examples of the noble savages who must exist if the myth of virgin land was true. But when he came to those tropical Gardens of Eden, the South Sea islands, he found the children of nature as corrupt as the men of civilization.

Melville's South Sea novels are essays in disenchantment which were to lead him to search for wisdom with the novelist who dared to criticize his fellow New Englanders for their commitment to utopia. He searched out Hawthorne. We have been aware of the intellectual friendship of these two men, but we have not, perhaps, realized how closely in theme Melville's masterpiece, *Moby-Dick,* expresses the philosophic and theological theme of *The Scarlet Letter.*

At first glance, the two novels seem wholly disparate. Melville is dealing with the American present; he is describing an isolated contemporary group, the Nantucket whalers. The theme of the central drama, nevertheless, is parallel to that of Hawthorne's; *Moby-Dick,* too, is an allegory of the myth of the New World Eden. Ishmael, like Arthur Dimmesdale, will achieve spiritual salvation by accepting his membership in "the sinful brotherhood of mankind." Captain Ahab is a Roger Chillingworth placed in command of the Pequod. And Melville's description of the horror of his rule exceeds the warnings inherent in the portrait of Hawthorne's Puritan ideologue. Driven by the sin of pride and dedicated to perfection, Ahab destroys himself and all those who follow him. Melville was more pessimistic, more gloomy about the Jacksonian generation than Hawthorne because he could see the pull of greed strengthening the sacrilegious quest for an earthly paradise.

Hawthorne's allegory took its form from his sense of New England history; Melville's emerged from his personal experience of flight to the sea to regain the innocence he saw disappearing in the eastern cities.

*Moby-Dick* begins with Ishmael retracing this path of retreat from the environment of New York City, which he senses as unnatural. The redemptive force of nature has been lost in this great center of commerce. Mankind, temporarily purified by the rural American landscape, is once more driven into disharmony by the artificial complexity of the city. But an unspoiled physical frontier washes against the wharves, the very symbols of the city's corrupt commercial life. And Ishmael sees in the vast watery emptiness which surrounds the crowded city a chance to re-establish harmony with nature: "Whenever I find myself growing grim about the mouth; whenever it is damp, drizzly November in my soul; whenever I find myself involuntarily pausing before coffin warehouses . . . then, I account it high time to get to sea as soon as I can. . . . almost all men in their degree, sometime or other, cherish very nearly the same feelings towards the ocean with me."

Ishmael is the representative Jacksonian American, attempting to recapitulate the exodus of his ancestors from the crowded cities of Europe, across the purifying waters of the ocean, to a promised land in the west where death, the badge of the ineradicable imperfection of the Eternal Adam, would no longer haunt mankind. Ishmael, like the average man, is not a fanatical believer in the religion of redemptive nature, but he will follow the prophets of this earthly religion if they promise there is profit to be made in the exodus. This symbolic citizen will ship to sea to profit from the exploitation of that nature which he supposedly worships.

The gentle Ishmael, the humble American, has emerged in Melville's portrait as a man driven to moral irresponsibility by his conceit. Even his religion of nature is a sham. He does not love nature; he only looks to it to find confirmation of the perfection he imagines to exist in his own soul. And so we are led through Ishmael to the myth of Narcissus.

For Melville, mankind has always been tempted to act the part of Narcissus and to project upon the surface of the most fundamental element in nature—water—its dream of inward perfection. Ishmael and his fellow Americans have looked upon nature, and there they have seen the reflection of their belief that they are earthly saints. Supposing themselves a saving remnant, they see no sins in their hearts which need to be washed away; water, become holy through the miracle of grace, cannot bring them to salvation; in their own prideful self-assessment, they have already achieved an earthly heaven.

Thus Melville introduces the theological framework that will give meaning to the drama of the novel. Americans, if they persist in their sin of pride, must like Narcissus find death in nature, death without redemption. Worshipping themselves, they have set up a false idol—nature—to mirror their self-love; they have lost the essential ingredient of the Christian faith, humility born of recognition of the Eternal Adam that is in all men.

It is within this philosophic and theological context that Ishmael reaches Nantucket Island to contract for a voyage. To escape from nature which has failed to fulfill its promise, he pushes on toward the ocean, toward what he believes is the remaining purity of nature and its promise of eternal harmony. And the closer he gets to the sea, the more Melville presents him with marine symbols of evil and death.

But Ishmael shrugs off these signs, safe in his knowledge that as an American he has an immortal soul that is predestined to transcend death. He listens to Father Mapple's sermon but he does not hear. Of what concern to an American is the old preacher's queer sermonizing about Jonah and the whale. Father Mapple begins by asking his congregation to consider the lesson which the story of Jonah teaches. This lesson, he admonishes, concerns the fate of man who willfully disobeys the command of God and sets up the false idol of self-worship. "If we obey God, we must disobey ourselves," the old minister says. "And it is this disobeying ourselves, wherein the hardness of obeying God consists." Ishmael does not understand this message, which is a warning against man's Narcissus-like quest for perfection, for that self-sufficiency which will make God's love and mercy irrelevant.

Nor does he understand Father Mapple's next point that "with this sin of disobedience in him, Jonah still further flouts at God, by seeking to flee from Him. He thinks that a ship made by men, will carry him into countries where God does not reign, but only the Captains of this earth." How can an American who is about to put to sea to escape the imperfections of his environment realize that the preacher has him in mind? But Jonah cannot escape God, and the sea is no refuge but a place of storm and terror, and Jonah is swallowed by the whale. He is then saved because "He feels that his dreadful punishment is just. He leaves all his deliverance to God, contenting himself with this, that in spite of all his pains and pangs, he will still look towards His holy temple. And here, shipmate, is true and faithful repentance; not clamourous for pardon, but grateful for punishment. . . . Sin not; but if you do, take heed to repent of it like Jonah."

Ishmael, however, lacks the sense of humility that might lead him into an understanding of this message which completes the theological structure of the novel. He will ship in the Pequod, captained by Ahab who is guilty of Jonah's sin of pride, and who "with this sin of disobedience in him . . . thinks that a ship made by men, will carry him into countries where God does not reign, but only the Captains of this earth." He is destined to be the lone survivor of the destruction of Ahab and his followers, which fulfills Father Mapple's warning; he will return to give witness before his countrymen to God's wrath against the sin of pride.

Ishmael's education and his salvation begin when he meets Queequeg the pagan harpooner from the South Seas. Queequeg had hoped to find perfection in Christian America: "But alas! The practices of whale men soon convinced him that even Christians could be both miserable and wicked; infinitely more so, than all his father's heathens. Arrived at last in old Sag Harbor; and seeing what the sailors did there; and then going on to Nantucket, and seeing how they spent their wages in that place also, poor Queequeg gave it up for lost. Thought he; it's a wicked world in all meridians; I'll die a pagan."

The irony of *The Scarlet Letter* was that the Puritans needed the sinful Hester and her child to save them from their sin of pride and to give them back their humanity. Now Melville pursues the same theme of irony by offering his fellow Americans salvation through the love of the sinful pagan, Queequeg. As Hawthorne called upon the Christian story to dramatize the unchristian lack of charity in the Puritans, so Melville uses Queequeg, given by his father, the king, to dwell as a humble workman among the sinners, as a reminder to the Jacksonians of how far they have strayed from Christian charity. The so-called Christians reject Queequeg with scorn. But he meets all their curses, their taunts and abuse with love. His simple philosophy is that "It's a mutual, joint-stock world, in all meridians. We cannibals must help these Christians." Always, Queequeg is ready to risk his life for his tormentors, as when he dives into the wintry Atlantic to rescue one of his attackers. Ultimately, he does die, loyal to the group of evil men who sail the Pequod, but his death brings salvation to Ishmael and through him, the possibility of salvation to all who will believe in his story.

Ishmael's first reaction to Queequeg is that of the self-righteous American who rejects all contact with sinful

strangers. Laughed at by his comrades when he is forced
to share the pagan's bed, he comes reluctantly to accept
him as a brother; for the first time in America, he has found
a man more generous than self-seeking, more motivated by
love of his fellow man than by lust for money. Queequeg's
goodness makes Ishmael aware of his own weakness; he is
willing to love his fellow man in spite of the weaknesses he
finds in them. And so it is a cannibal who saves Ishmael by
teaching him the Golden Rule, the necessity of love and
brotherhood in a world that is a democracy of sinners.
"Heaven have mercy on us all—Presbyterians and Pagans
alike—for we are somehow dreadfully cracked about the
head."

Ishmael now has new eyes to see beneath the surface
of American complacency. He becomes aware of the greed
which makes American Christians so hypocritical. The
Pequod is owned by the pious Quaker captains Bildad and
Peleg, who are leaders of the spiritual life of Nantucket. It
is Peleg who stops Bildad's preaching to Queequeg, with
the practical advice, "Pious harpooners never make good
voyagers," and it is Bildad who guides the Pequod out of
the harbor to save the pilot fee. These two good captains
turn their ship over to Captain Ahab on Christmas day,
aware that Ahab is a blasphemous believer in some dark
faith, but certain, too, that his harsh discipline guarantees a
good profit.

The piloting of the Pequod out of the harbor would
seem to be, for Melville, symbolic of the American situation.
The men who left Europe for the New World followed
captains who promised both innocence and profit. But ultimately, the ship may fall into the hands of a fanatic who
can cleverly play upon the greed of his crew to keep them
disciplined while he leads them to their death in a mad
quest for impossible perfection.

Hawthorne had introduced Roger Chillingworth to
Massachusetts as a man who had been the captive of savages

in the wilderness—a symbol of Chillingworth's pact with
the devil, which separated him from the ranks of humanity.
Ishmael is only allowed a suspicion of the identity of the
black shadows which slip into the hold of the Pequod on
the night of her departure. Ultimately, he learns that the
devil has provided Ahab with a special crew for his whale
boat to sustain his sacrilegious quest for revenge against the
white whale. But at the outset, he cannot understand the
opaque warning of the mad beggar, Elizah, who asks him,
"Have ye shipped in her? . . . Anything down there about
your souls?" He has not escaped far enough from the complacency of America to define the practicality of Peleg and
Bildad as itself a fanaticism that can lead to death; he cannot see that the ranting of prophets, like Elizah, is only the
truth of common sense on which a continuing life must be
built.

For Ahab, it is not man who has faltered in the quest
for perfection; it is nature which has failed to provide the
environment in which man's quest for perfection could fulfill
itself. The mystery which Chillingworth pledged to banish
from the universe still haunted his Jacksonian descendants.
These nineteenth-century Americans had not followed Arthur
Dimmesdale to the self-identification with the Eternal Adam;
they had not accepted their burden of guilt. Now their
leader was the mad fanatic, Ahab, who cursed God for
failing to give him perfection and who renewed Roger Chillingworth's pledge to rid the world of mystery.

"The White Whale swam before him as the monomaniac
incarnation of all those malicious agencies which some deep
men feel eating them, till they are left living on with half a
heart and half a lung. That intangible malignity which has
been from the beginning; to whose dominion even the
modern Christians ascribe one half of the world . . . Ahab
. . . pitted himself, all mutilated, against it. All that most
maddens and torments; all that stirs up the lees of things, all
truth with malice in it . . . all evil, to crazy Ahab, were

visibly personified and practically available in Moby Dick. He piled upon the whale's white hump the sum of all the general rage and hate felt by his whole race from Adam down. . . . Is it that by its indefiniteness it [the White Whale] shadows forth the heartless voids and immensities of the universe, and thus stabs us from behind with the thought of annihilation, when beholding the white depths of the milky way? . . . And when we consider the other theory of the natural philosophers, that all other early hues— every stately or lovely emblazoning—the sweet tinges of sunset skies and woods; yea, and the gilded velvets of butterflies, and the butterfly cheeks of young girls; all these are but subtle deceits, not actually inherent in substances, but only laid on from without; so that all deified Nature absolutely paints like the harlot, whose allurements cover nothing but the charnel-house within . . . and of all these things the albino whale was the symbol. Wonder ye then at the fiery hunt?"

Thus Ahab confesses that the essential purpose of the voyage is metaphysical; he is dedicated to wreak vengeance on Moby-Dick and rid the world of mystery. His three mates are incapable of deflecting him from his purpose. Flask, the third mate, is too mediocre. The second mate, Stubb, has ability but is a moral and spiritual illiterate; for him, life is experienced on the single level of practicality. He cannot see the blasphemy of Ahab's plan. Whatever hope of saving the ship lies with the first mate, Starbuck, who is capable of moral and spiritual insight. A pious Quaker, a devoted family man, he is horrified when he learns of Ahab's quest for vengeance. "My soul is more than matched; she's over-manned; and by a madman. . . . I think I see his impious end; but feel that I must help him to it. . . . Horrible old man!"

Starbuck's weakness is that of "mere unaided virtue or right-mindedness." Just as Melville prepares our understanding of Ahab's sin in Father Mapple's sermon, so he also clarifies Starbuck's situation. At the end of his sermon, the preacher had added a second lesson to Jonah's story. The Almighty instructed Jonah "to preach the Truth to the face of Falsehood! . . . This, shipmate, this is that other lesson; and woe to that pilot of the living God who slights it. Woe to him whom this world charms from Gospel duty! Woe to him who seeks to pour oil upon the waters when God has brewed them into a gale! Woe to him who seeks to please rather than to appall!"

Starbuck is faced by a man of iron will who appeals in sacrilegious rites to the devil for the superhuman strength needed to destroy Moby-Dick. Against Ahab's devil worship, he can only preach profits. He does not "preach the truth in the face of falsehood" because it is he "whom this world charms from Gospel duty." And so the moral and spiritual leadership he offers the crew reads like this, "I come here to hunt whales, not my commander's vengeance. How many barrels will thy vengeance yield thee even if thou gettest it, Captain Ahab? . . . Sperm, sperm's the play! This at least is duty; duty and profit hand in hand." Starbuck cannot challenge Ahab on spiritual grounds because his first commitment is to the rewards of this world. He believes that he has security as long as he does his duty. He sees the evil in Ahab but hopes it will disappear under the discipline of the ship's work. Cut off from God by his concern for profits, he can only depend on "mere unaided virtue or right-mindedness."

It is Ishmael who makes Melville's critical comment on this pious American faith in the inevitable triumph of the virtuous and practical man. On watch one night, he is overcome by a vision of overpowering terror and he attempts to escape from its lingering horror by echoing the American belief in natural goodness: "Look not too long in the face of the fire, Oh, man! . . . believe not the artificial fire, when its redness makes all things look ghastly. Tomorrow in the natural sun, the skies will be bright; those who glared like devils in the forking flames, the morn will show in far other, at least gentler, relief; the glorious, glorious, glad sun." Evil, for the American, is only appearance, not substance. The American is invulnerable. For Ishmael, as for Starbuck, the darkness of Ahab's madness will disappear under the bright reasonableness of the ship's discipline.

But then he breaks from this traditional incantation of optimism to accept the existence of evil. "Nevertheless the sun hides not Virginia's Dismal Swamp, nor Rome's accursed Campagna, nor wide Sahara, nor all the millions of miles of deserts and of griefs beneath the moon. The sun hides not the ocean, which is the dark side of this earth, and which is two thirds of this earth. So, therefore, that mortal man who hath more of joy than sorrow in him, that mortal man cannot be true—not true."

Ishmael has made his break with the symbol of redemptive water which has haunted him from the beginning of the novel. Accepting his mortality, he will no longer be the follower of Narcissus, and will thus escape the fate of Narcissus. Rejecting perfection, he asserts that the dignity of man comes from living with an imperfect physical environment which cannot redeem him but can provide him with a challenge that can uplift him. "And there is a Catskill eagle in some souls that can alike dive into the blackest gorges, and soar out of them again and become invisible in the sunny spaces. And even if he forever flies within the Gorge, that Gorge is in the mountains; so that even in his lowest swoop the mountain eagle is still higher than other birds upon the plain, even though they soar."

Ishmael accepts man's fate as similar to the eagle's. It is not a limiting fate; rather it gives man the freedom to live and die with dignity. Ishmael has finally understood the full meaning of Father Mapple's sermon. And so once again, we must return to the preacher's words to find the concluding theme of the novel. His last admonition to the congregation was, "And eternal delight and deliciousness will be his, who coming to lay him down, can say with his final breath —O Father . . . here I die. I have striven to be thine, more than to be this world's, or mine own. Yet this is nothing; I leave eternity to Thee; for what is man that he should live out the lifetime of his God?"

For Ahab, if man is to be free, he must have the freedom to escape from death. In a moving scene just before he meets the White Whale, Ahab suddenly reveals his continuing human instincts. Reminiscing with Starbuck about his youth, he seems about to transcend his preoccupation with revenge when he cries out, "Why this strife of the chase. . . . I feel deadly faint, bowed, and humped, as though I were Adam, staggering beneath the piled centuries since Paradise. . . . Close! Stand close to me Starbuck; let me look into a human eye . . . this is the magic glass, man; I see my wife and my child in thine eye. . . . What is it, what nameless, inscrutable, unearthly thing is it; what cozening, hidden lord and master, and cruel, remorseless emperor commands me; that against all natural lovings and longings, I do so keep pushing, and crowding, and jamming myself on all the time?" But then he returns to his savage self, and his anger is monumental. "I am driven," he shouts, because he is not free: "By heaven, man, we are turned round and round in this world, like yonder windlass, and Fate is the handspike." What does Ahab mean by Fate? It is death: "Aye, toil we how we may, we all sleep at last in the field."

So Ahab, to escape death, rushes on to death. For three hate-filled days, he has his crew hunt Moby-Dick. Always the whale swims away from his curses. But on the third day, the whale turns on his tormentors, destroys the Pequod, and drags Ahab into the depths. The ship and crew sinks into the sea without hope of resurrection.

In the epilogue of a single page, Melville quotes from Job, "And I only am escaped alone to tell thee." Ishmael has alone survived the disaster to return to tell his tale. Would his fellow Americans understand what he has wit-

nessed? Would they observe the possible parallel between
Jonah and Ahab, between the fate of America and the fate
of the Pequod? Job accepted the inscrutable ways of God,
the mystery of the universe. Ishmael survives because he has
learned from Queequeg to find hope in symbols of mystery
and death.

On the voyage, Queequeg had become seriously ill and
had asked for a coffin to be made for him. During the re-
mainder of his illness, he had slept in it and when he re-
covered, he continued to use it as a sea chest and to carve
upon it copies of the tattoos which adorned his body. For
those who read closely, Melville has carefully established
the relationship between the mystery of redemption and this
symbol of death: "And this tattooing has been the work of a
departed prophet and seer of his island, who, by these hiero-
glyphic marks, had written out on his body a complete
theory of the heavens and the earth, and a mystical treatise
on the art of attaining truth; so that Queequeg in his own
proper person was a riddle to unfold; a wondrous work in
one volume; but whose mysteries not even himself could
read, though his own live heart beat against them; and these
mysteries were, therefore, in the end to moulder away with
the living parchment whereon they were inscribed, and so
be unsolved to the last."

This prince of peace might not understand the ways
of his creator but he died as he lived, accepting his fate,
delivered from evil because he had faith. He had a faith
which kept him from searching for earthly perfection, from
attempting to escape his humanity, but permitted him to
live in harmony with Father Mapple's prayer, "I leave
eternity to Thee for what is man that he should live out the
lifetime of his God." In the end it is Queequeg's coffin, engraved with the pagan's mysterious theology, which comes
up from the depths to provide a life raft for Ishmael.

Would Americans comprehend that Ahab and his crew
had disappeared into the deep because they believed in their

own perfection? Could they understand that Ishmael alone
was saved because he had been converted by Queequeg to
the acceptance of his identity with the Eternal Adam whose
salvation was not in this world? History tells us they did not
learn. Instead, with the seemingly satisfactory conclusion to
the problems that had caused the Civil War, the vast
majority of Americans congratulated themselves on the
final completion of the American Eden. The next generation
of American novelists would reach maturity still believing
in the existence of the American Adam. The dramatic theme
of their novels from 1870 to 1900 lies in their discovery that
the Eternal Adam yet lived in the hearts of their countrymen, and there was no Garden.

# II

---

# THE REALISTS

---

*Mark Twain*
*William Dean Howells*
*Henry James*

# 1

Mark Twain was the first important novelist from the valley of democracy, and in his early years he shared fully in the national optimism of post-Civil War America. His reading of history reinforced his faith in the meaning of the United States. From the writings of the great English Whig historians, he learned that history was the record of progress which in turn was the story of liberty. Once, they wrote, in classical times, men had lived in dignity and freedom under the guidance of reason. But this golden period succumbed to the Dark Ages. Men had become slaves to the superstition of the Church, and to the power of feudal kings and lords whose tyranny the church justified.

Then gradually, according to this historical narrative, during the Renaissance and Reformation men began to break from the tyranny of superstition and absolute government. By the eighteenth century, Europe had achieved a state of Enlightenment. Now free from the authority of priests and lords and kings, the individual was able to follow the promptings of his own reason. But Mark Twain could not believe that progress and liberty had culminated in eighteenth-century England. For him, vestiges of the medieval past clearly prevailed in England and France even after the French Revolution.

It was only in America that perfect liberty had been achieved by 1800. The presidency of Jefferson had marked the achievement of the American covenant with nature which guaranteed every citizen freedom from the theological chains of the Middle Ages. Perfect simplicity, perfect harmony, perfect stability—these were the characteristics of Jefferson's republic as Twain saw them. Here history as progress was fulfilled. In 1865, Twain agreed with Bancroft's analysis of the national situation in 1830: the human condition was transcended. From now on, men in the New World would live as reborn Adams in timeless tranquility. True, this Eden had been marred until 1865 by the continued presence of feudalism in the South. But the successful conclusion of the Civil War had purged the country of that final flaw and now the peace of the Jeffersonian republic would prevail forever more.

Mark Twain went abroad immediately after the Civil War, seemingly secure in his faith in the stable existence of the American Eden. The reports he sent back in *The Innocents Abroad* were predicated on an American reading public that would share his laughter and his tears at the comic and tragic human condition in Europe. But why did Twain feel the need to reaffirm his faith in the innocence of his nation? And the plain folks at home who avidly read his reports, why did they need to be reassured that Europe was more unhappy than the United States?

Southern feudalism had collapsed only to reveal a more dangerous threat to the simplicity of the Jeffersonian republic—industrial capitalism. The nation, caught up in the fantastic development of factory and city unleashed by the war itself, could not pause to analyze its furious drive away from agrarian simplicity. How could Americans remain loyal to the Jeffersonian ideal, even as they plundered the land they supposedly revered to make room for steel mills and tenements?

Somehow Mark Twain managed to find an explanation as he turned his face away from the West toward Europe. He had to believe the machine was a complement not a contradiction to nature. Most Europeans, he wrote home from abroad, lived in poverty and ignorance because they did not have the spirit of enterprise. There were, however, good Europeans who, patterning themselves after Americans, were learning to build railroads. Soon Western technology would provide the path to the promised land of liberty for these backward people.

Perhaps Twain was in such need of reassurance that history was the progressive development of liberty, and that its motive force was business enterprise and technology, because he was so aware of the corruption which was accompanying the building of the urban-industrial society in America. When he shared in the writing of *The Gilded Age* with Charles Warner, he bitterly criticized the destruction of the old republic. "The eight years in America from 1860 to 1868 uprooted institutions . . . changed the politics of a people, transformed the social life of half the country." The authors were appalled by the rootlessness of the new generation. Against its lack of standards, its corroding materialism, its irresponsible selfishness, they contrasted the stability, the sobriety, the virtue of the Jeffersonian village world and the middle-class aristocracy of the Jeffersonian cities. The frightening implication of this change for Twain must have been the fact that the most corrupt people described in the book were from the West—Dilworthy, Hawkins, Sellers, and Laura. All the evidence pointed to the contradictory role of the new economic forces in Europe and America. Liberating and purifying in the Old World, they seemed imprisoning and corrupting in the New.

By the beginning of the 1870's Mark Twain had reached a dilemma. He believed that history must be progressive and man energetic and practical. But he also believed that the purpose of progress was to liberate man from the confining institutions and traditions of the Middle Ages so that he could live in harmony with nature. He saw the creative inventiveness of man as the method by which the useless past was to be swept into the ashcan of history. However, since the Jeffersonian republic was established in the opening decades of the nineteenth century, and progress had reached its culmination in the liberty of the American state of nature, there was no need for man to be destructively creative. Destructively creative—here was the very heart of Twain's dilemma. He had always thought of the practical inventions of modern man as weapons for the destruction of the superstitions of the medieval church and the institutions of medieval monarchy. But in the America of 1870, there were no vestiges of the Dark Ages to be destroyed. Progress, as the creative destructiveness of industrialism, could now only lead Americans away from the Jeffersonian Eden. Were Americans in the name of headlong progress building a railroad that would lead them straight back to the abyss of the Dark Ages? How could the Jeffersonian arcadia be preserved?

Twain's first answer was pure transcendence of the problem. He wrote *Tom Sawyer*, where the real world was no longer that of the troubled man but the romance of the innocent child. Tom Sawyer lives his private dreams within the dreamlike setting of St. Petersburg, nestled within its natural bower of river and hills. When Twain wrote that "Cardiff hill, beyond the village and above it, was green with vegetation, and it lay just far enough away to seem a De-

lectable Land, dreamy, reposeful, and inviting," he was
describing his nostalgic escape from the harsh realities of
the Gilded Age. Momentarily, he could pretend that this
dream was the true foundation of his country and that the
innocence of these children could become the model of
adult behavior. Grown men must become like Tom Sawyer
and reject the practical creativity, the ambition, and the
selfishness of the so-called real world of progress; they must
always remain in the timeless world of nature.

But if Americans have refused to live in timeless harmony with nature, if they have not remained innocent children, is the fault only in the human heart? Or was nature also
at fault for failing to redeem man and lift him above his
inherent weakness? What is the significance of Tom's discovery of gold buried deep in the heart of nature? The cave,
which had served Tom as a refuge from the disharmony of
the adult world, initiates him into the terror of that environment when he encounters Indian Joe. And then the gold
forces him finally into the society of his elders with the
burden of practicality and responsibility it imposes upon
him.

Twain's agonized voice can be heard. There is time
where there should be timelessness; the virgin land had
failed to save Americans from the mortality of history. Tom
Sawyer would grow to manhood; he would use his gold to
further his ambitions. Abandoning the romantic dream of
childhood, he too would become the practical man of this
world.

Like Melville's Ishmael, Twain turned away from land
to water as the final symbol of unspoiled and still redemptive nature. If only America were located in the wilderness
of the ocean like the paradise of Pitcairn Island where people
"lived in a deep Sabbath tranquility, far from the world and
its ambitions and vexations, and neither knowing nor caring
what was going on in the mighty empires that lie beyond

their ocean solitudes."* If ships touched occasionally with "news of bloody battles, devastating epidemics, fallen thrones, and ruined dynasties," they sailed away again leaving the inhabitants "to retire into their peaceful dreams . . . once more." But the oceans did not isolate America; they connected it with the historical civilizations of Europe and Asia.

The faith of the people of the United States in redemption by nature had focused on the valley of democracy as the citadel of the American Garden. And the heart of the valley was the river, the Mississippi. Escaping from the land which had failed him, Twain fled to the river to find surcease from the discordant rhythms of progress. Although ambitious men changed its banks, the river itself could not be altered. Here was a symbol of nature that flowed with an everlasting sameness, where man's dream of innocence could find constant renewal and confirmation. Here was Twain's last chance to provide immortality for the American Adam.

Shorebound men had not achieved their dream of harmony with nature, he wrote in *Life on the Mississippi*, because they had not dreamed the right dream. Europeans, crossing the Atlantic and settling the eastern seaboard, had not transcended the medieval past. Nor had the pioneers, crossing the Appalachians into the great interior valley, abandoned the superstitions of Europe. Indeed, they had established a grotesque caricature of those dark centuries, which reached to the edge of the river itself. Most of the settlements along the Mississippi, Twain wrote, were part of that southern culture which was only a primitive frontier expression of medieval civilization. The South of 1860 was feudal, its values were those of "war, murder . . . the duel, repudiation and massacre. . . . Ignorance, intolerance, egotism, self-assertion." Its people read Sir Walter Scott, admired

*Quoted in Roger Salomon, *Twain and the Image of History* (Yale, 1961).

his "fantastic heroes," and built their state capitols like that
in Baton Rouge as "a little sham castle."

In *Life on the Mississippi*, Twain now denied that progress had reached fulfillment in Jefferson's time; the medieval
past had prevailed in America until the Civil War. There
was still a positive role then for the destructive creativity
of industrialism in the United States. Progress was not so
much moving away from the covenant with nature of 1800,
as moving toward a covenant which had not yet been sealed
between the American people and the ultimate shrine of
nature, the Mississippi River.

Twain wrote with enthusiasm of the destruction of the
old decadent culture by the forces of business enterprise and
technology. "The signs are that the next twenty years will
bring some noteworthy changes in the valley, in the direction of increased population and wealth and in the intellectual advancement and the liberalizing of opinion which
go naturally with these." One finds, he continued, "All the
enlivening signs of the presence of active, energetic, intelligent, prosperous, practical nineteenth-century populations
which don't dream; they work." Only progress through
business enterprise and technology could destroy the evil
heritage of the past.

But Twain failed to persuade himself that his argument
was sound. Running through *Life on the Mississippi* is the
disturbing recognition that creative, technical change was
not only destroying the feudal dream of southern society; it
was moving on to the river itself, and defiling its innocence.
This is the poignant theme which dominates the conclusion
where Twain describes the river's loss of autonomy as it falls
under the polluting control of a new business and machine-
oriented civilization.

The controlling allegory is that of the river pilot as the
authentic American Adam. Twain affirmed that he "loved
the profession far better than any I have followed since and

I took a measureless pride in it. The reason is plain; a pilot, in those days, was the only unfettered and entirely independent human being that lived on the earth. . . . In truth, every man and woman and child has a master, and worries and frets in servitude; but in the day I write of, the Mississippi pilot had none." The pilot, alone among men, was not ruled by the laws of civilization; he had achieved organic harmony with the river and was guided by its laws. Intuitively he sensed his course. He did not impose his will on the river but lived by accepting its demands.

Now the engineers have come to conquer the Mississippi in the name of civilization. They work to remove the snags, to dredge and mark the channels. They aim to force the river to run within their charts, and replace the natural pilot with that figure of artificial culture, the captain, who works from man-made charts and guideposts. Civilization has defeated the American Adam, who had lived with the innocence of a child in his simple dependence on the natural river. But now the river has been imprisoned by the business-dominated towns and cities which line its banks.

And so Twain turned back to fiction to recapture his faith in progress. In his novels, he could reverse time and return to that moment when innocence had defeated corruption, when boys had conquered men. Fleeing his beloved river where realism was overcoming romance, he turned to the historical fantasy of *The Prince and the Pauper,* where romance was to emerge victorious over realism. In this historical novel about boys, it is obvious that Twain was searching for confirmation of his faith in man's instinctive goodness: man comes into the world as an innocent child and is taught to be evil.

Just as Jefferson's republic was the moment in time when the individual was most free, so medieval civilization had marked the nadir of human history, when all the weight of accumulated evil suffocated man's spirit. Twain returned to this heart of darkness to find hope in the figures of two boys, Tom Canty and Prince Edward. Tom Canty was born in the horror of a London slum in the middle of the sixteenth century. His father was a drunk, a thief, a murderer. But the boy rejects his father's attempt to mold him after his own image. Instinctively, he loves his fellow men and rejects his father's code; he dreams of escape from the adult jungle. If only he were the young Prince Edward, able to avoid all the ugliness of this world of vicious men within the safety of his castle walls. But the Prince, too, dreams of escape from his father's world of tyranny and savagery. As king, he would have to act without love or mercy or justice toward his subjects. Inherently good, like Tom Canty, Edward also refuses to accept maturity on his father's terms.

As it happens, the two boys not only feel alike, they also resemble each other physically. When chance brings about their reversal of roles, Tom finds himself living in the castle and Edward in the slum. Tom learns that princes and kings are not free and Edward sees the horrible plight of his subjects. United at the conclusion of the story, the two boys are formidable in their insight and knowledge, strong in their still uncorrupted virtue, and invincible in their dedication to end the stupidity, the injustice, the savagery of medieval law and custom. Thus do these inspired innocents slay the dragon of social evil, and free their people to live by the innate goodness which exists in every man's heart as the legacy of his childhood.

Mark Twain could take no lasting comfort in this fairy tale. He could not escape the realization that Jefferson's republic had failed to redeem mankind—that Americans of the middle of the nineteenth century still expressed all the selfishness, cruelty, and evil of the nobility and peasantry of the Dark Ages. The childish optimism of *The Prince and the Pauper* needed to be replaced by the mature pessimism of *Huckleberry Finn*. This novel is perhaps the most poignant expression of any American's loss of hope for the unique destiny of his nation as that sanctuary in which mankind was to experience a rebirth and to regain Eden.

Twain began *Huckleberry Finn,* his greatest artistic triumph, even before he had concluded *The Prince and the Pauper.* In many ways, Huck is a parallel to Tom Canty. He is a prisoner of the feudalism of the early nineteenth century, and his father, too, is a drunk, a thief, a murderer. But Huck, like Tom Canty, can transcend his culture to express the goodness of his heart. Brought up in a society that is at best callous and at worst cruel, he can sympathize with the sufferings of all humans, even a Negro slave. Huck, however, will find no prince to destroy feudalism, only a Tom Sawyer who ultimately accepts Southern society. And he will find no answering innocence in the hearts of the common man. He will discover that it is innate evil and not the social heritage which creates disharmony in the world. In the nineteenth century, unlike the sixteenth, there can only be an unhappy ending to a book for boys who refuse to be men.

The novel begins with a scathing criticism of the kind of romanticism on which he had built *The Prince and the Pauper.* Tom Sawyer and his friends are living in a make-believe world of childish romance while Huck Finn is being civilized by the town aristocracy. Like Tom Canty, he learns that there is no freedom in the citadels of the upper class. Caught between the reality of his degraded father and this new genteel degradation, he has no alternative but to flee. As he paddles out to Jackson's Island in the heart of the Mississippi to hide in the cave in this last island of virgin land, preserved in its purity by the magic potency of the uncivilized river, we follow him with the tragic eyes of his creator, who has been there before. For Twain, by 1885, not only has virgin land failed to redeem the European but even the river has been unable to defeat the artificial culture of civilization. The idea of nature as a redeeming force has proved to be a bankrupt myth; the disharmony of European civilization had blended with the disharmony of American nature.

On the island, Huck discovers the runaway slave, Jim, and there these exiles from corrupt society recapture the dream of natural brotherhood which had been shared by Deerslayer and Chingachgook a century before. But Twain, who has passionately loved the myth of nature, could not imitate Cooper's calm symbolism in which the fruitfulness of nature had gradually faded away. And no aspect of nature was more cruel in its deceptiveness than the river itself, which had held the last promise of timeless harmony.

*snake too like adam + Eve*

Huck and Jim have to abandon their hideout, which has failed them as a refuge. But even before they can take to their raft, the flooding, rampaging river brings death to the island. Later Huck will learn that the faceless corpse was his father. He will learn, beyond Tom Canty's and Prince Edward's knowledge, that there is no escape from the fathers, no new beginning, no recovery of lost innocence. The river promises not life but death; this is the burden of Huck's initiation into reality as the river carries them southward. Enshrouded in fog, it carries them past Cairo, Illinois, where they had hoped to move up the Ohio River to freedom. As we see the clear water of this northern river being absorbed into the dark currents of the Mississippi, we wonder if this is not the inescapable path of history from light to darkness, if it is not impossible for Huck and Jim to escape the judgment of time which suddenly finds symbolic expression in the black and ominous flow of water.

Eventually, the raft is taken over by two confidence men intent on exploiting the towns along the way. Complicity, not innocence, is the role of the river now as the duke and king prove the utter gullibility of human nature by stealing the inheritance of the Wilks sisters. Huck's pilgrimage ends in disillusionment and despair in Louisiana.

Instead of leading to the boundless freedom of the sea, the river loses itself in the constricted backwaters of this stronghold of slavery where Jim is put back into shackles.

If Twain has been ruthless with Huck and with himself throughout this pilgrim's progress, he has saved the cruelest moment of revelation for the climax of his story. As Huck despairs of rescuing Jim, Tom Sawyer surprisingly appears and immediately agrees to help free Jim from captivity. Huck, who has wrestled so desperately with his own conscience before his complete commitment to Jim's cause, cannot believe that a law-abiding boy like Tom, whose only rebellion against society has taken the form of historical fantasy, will now act from an instinct of brotherly love against the conscience of the community. But Tom seems eager to use his romantic imagination to construct a workable, if elaborate plan, full of Gothic detail, that can free Jim.

When the burlesque drama is successfully concluded with Jim's escape, the Negro voluntarily returns to captivity in order to get medical attention for Tom, who has been slightly wounded in the flight. Triumphantly, Tom tells Huck that all is not lost because he had come down the river to find Jim who has been freed by his owner. He had kept Jim in needless captivity, had forced him to risk his life in order to fulfill his own need to live in a realm of perpetual fantasy in which innocent boys conquer the forces of evil.

Huck again has no recourse but flight. Like Leatherstocking, he will go to the unsettled land of the Far West, even though he knows that this last frontier will fail him and he will be forced back into the society he hates. No wonder when, in Twain's notebooks, the grown-up Huck returns from the West, he has become a madman.

With the writing of *Huckleberry Finn,* Mark Twain had purged himself of any nostalgic hopes he might still have nurtured for the redemption of humanity in America by contact with nature. In *A Connecticut Yankee in King Arthur's Court*, he showed that he had lost all hope for progress through business enterprise and technological achievement.

Twain's Yankee is the epitome of nineteenth-century technological skill and practicality. Transported back in time to King Arthur's court, he sees that Arthur and his knights are prisoners of supersitition which reduces them to the level of "big children." Aristocracy and common people alike are prisoners of "that awful power, the Roman Catholic Church. In two or three little centuries, it had converted a nation of men into a nation of worms! The Church had brought Englishmen to a completely subservient and passive level of patience, resignation, an uncomplaining acceptance of whatever fate befalls them in this life." The Yankee figures that if he can break the power of the Church to control education, there will be an automatic renaissance born of man's innate intelligence. And so he proceeds to build schools and factories to make the people free, happy, and prosperous. Trained to independence and rationality by business enterprise and technological efficiency, they can then destroy all restrictive institutions and live in natural harmony guided by their instinctive goodness.

When warfare breaks out among the knights as they quarrel over that heart of the modern economy, the stock market, the churchmen seize the opportunity to march against their enemy, the Yankee. But he is confident. After all, he has the technology of the nineteenth century on his side; he has people trained to nineteenth-century rationality. When he is told by Clarence, "We haven't sixty faithful left," he shouts, "What are you saying? Our schools, our colleges, our vast workshops, our . . ." And Clarence replies, "When those knights come, those establishments will empty themselves and go over to the enemy. Did you think you had educated the superstititions out of those people?"

The Yankee, with only a small band of faithful, can

destroy the hosts of the advancing knights with his modern guns and electrified barbed wire. But when the battle is over and the enemy is destroyed, he finds himself a prisoner of the enemy dead. Surely, Twain's controlling metaphor here is that while modern civilization has destroyed the medieval past, it has so trapped man within his artificial inventions that he is cut off from the life-giving force of nature. The Yankee's conclusion, his final initiation into reality, is that he can never escape from civilization of some form because of his own innate irrationality. "What a donkey I was! Toward the end of the week, I began to get this large and disenchanting fact through my head. . . . Why even the very men who had lately been slaves were in the 'righteous cause,' and glorifying it, praying for it . . . just like all the other commoners. Imagine such human stuff as this; conceive of this folly!"

When the Yankee is discovered wandering in modern England, the capital of the industrial revolution, he is insane. Betrayed by reality, his faith in progress shattered, madness remains the only protection for his faith in innocence. When we recall that in Twain's notebooks, Huck returns from the West with his intelligence destroyed, we are aware that the author has exhausted his final intellectual argument against his own belief that historical change now meant the inexorable degradation of American democracy.

Neither nature nor technology could save America. Must Twain then join his fictional creatures and transcend historical disharmony by escaping the laws of reason? Before he accepted the madness of despair, he would make a last attempt to save himself through a divine madness, a miraculous madness of hope. There is no greater irony in American cultural history than Mark Twain's supplication at the feet of a medieval saint for a miracle which could lift the curse of advancing doom from the face of the nation.

With all his heart, he explained that his biographical study of Joan of Arc "is to be a serious book. . . . It means more to me than anything I have ever undertaken." He needed to believe that regression was not inexorable, and he searched for an historical instance when innocence had survived in the midst of corruption, an historical character who had led a crusade against the infamous established social structure of the adult world. Such was Joan of Arc. But Twain could only worship her memory and stand in awe before the record of her brief existence. She is unique, he wrote, her personality "is one to be reverently studied, loved, and marveled at, but not to be wholly understood and accounted for by even the most searching analysis. . . . All the rules fail in this girl's case. In the world's history, she stands alone—quite alone. . . . She rose above the limitations and infirmities of our human nature."

This is why Twain's discovery of Joan could not save him from despair but only plunge him deeper into darkness. Joan could defeat the institutional power of feudal Europe on the battlefield but she could not destroy the wickedness in the hearts of men. This was the knowledge that had driven Huck and the Yankee mad.

Every champion that Mark Twain had sent against the medieval enemy had been crushed except the fantasy figures of Tom Canty and Prince Edward. Now in the 1890's, he would send no further heroes against the foe. He had begun his war to defend America against the encroachment of medieval darkness, believing that mankind was inherently innocent and had been corrupted only by the artificial institutions and traditions of the past. He had believed that since Americans had achieved total liberation from that past at the beginning of the nineteenth century, they could henceforth live in total peace, stability, and harmony with nature. But instead of living as the innocent children of nature, Americans had begun to conquer and exploit their physical environment and to create a new civilization, urban and industrial.

Twain had come to see that it is man who creates

civilization rather than civilization creating man. It is man who imposes evil upon his social environment rather than the other way around. No one could stop Americans from replacing nature with civilization. I am living, Twain wrote, "in the noonday glory of the Great Civilization, a witness of its gracious and beautiful youth, witness of its middle-time of giant power, sordid splendor and mean ambitions, and witness also of its declining vigor and the first stages of its hopeless retreat before the resistless forces which itself had created and which were to destroy it. . . . wonderful in scientific marvels . . . in material inflation which it calls Progress. . . . It is a civilization which has destroyed the simplicity and repose of life; replaced its contentment, its poetry, its soft romance-dreams and visions with money-fever." Twain's final vision of the American future is a holo-caust created by an engineer-dictator who destroys his nation and himself with the finest product of its science and technology—the ultimate weapon. The nation will commit suicide in the name of progress.

Driven to the final extremity, Twain now, like Ahab, turns to the devil for help in escaping his unbearable burden of mortality. He asks deliverance through the teachings of *The Mysterious Stranger.*

The devil first forces him to acknowledge the truth which he already secretly knows: "In five or six thousand years, five or six high civilizations have risen, flourished, commanded the wonder of the world, then faded out and disappeared, and not one of them except the latest ever invented any sweeping and adequate way to kill people. . . . The first man was a hypocrite and a coward, qualities which have not yet failed in his line; it is the foundation upon which all civilizations have been built."

But then Satan offers him an escape from these truths. "Are you so unobservant as not to have found that sanity and happiness are an impossible combination?" Gratefully,

Twain grasped at this means of transcending the wheel of history, that irresistible cycle which was leading Americans out of a natural paradise back into the terrors of time. If one accepted satanic madness, one learned that these apparently substantial patterns of historical development dissolved into the fancies of man's imagination. There was no reality outside of imagination. Everything was a dream, and a man was always free to dream. Gratefully, Twain surrenders his historical intelligence as he joins in agreement with Satan: "It is all a dream—a grotesque and foolish dream."

# 2

William Dean Howells, like Mark Twain, was born in the valley of democracy a generation before the Civil War. He, too, was to grow to manhood assuming that the war, in smashing southern feudalism, had made the nation permanently safe for the American Adam. His novels of the last decades of the nineteenth century, focused, like Twain's, on the discovery of a disharmonious American reality which violently contradicted the ideal of an American Eden.

Born in Ohio, Howells was more explicitly indoctrinated with the vision of agrarian simplicity than was Twain. He was taught to accept personal responsibility for the ideals of individual freedom by his father, who had abandoned a job because it conflicted with his principles and taken his family into a communitarian society to avoid any compromise. Later, when the elder Howells found that he could link his ideals with the new Republican Party of the 1850's, the son threw himself into his father's new cause and achieved recognition by writing a successful campaign biography of Abraham Lincoln. This success led to economic security when the new administration rewarded him with a consulship in Venice. Now the once poor boy from rural Ohio could make an advantageous marriage to a New England girl who had important family connections.

When Howells returned to the United States in 1865, Republicanism and nationalism had triumphed. Slavery, the southern aristocracy, the last vestiges of corrupting Old World history were extirpated from the American landscape. With the publication of his book *Venetian Life*, the bright young man from the Midwest won the attention of one east coast editor after another. A good job in New York with *The Nation* was followed by a better with *The Atlantic* in Boston. In 1871 the young friend of Lowell, Fiske, Agassiz, and Norton became the editor of *The Atlantic*. How far and how fast the poor boy from Ohio had come! Smug and complacent about the perfection of America and its moral and technological superiority to Europe, Howells was editing the most important journal of opinion in the most important city in the most important country.

But, like Mark Twain, and at the same time, he began to doubt his assumption of America's superiority to Europe; he began to see the possibility of conflict between economic progress and the security of Jeffersonian morality. More and more articles came across his editor's desk, like those of Henry Demarest Lloyd, which cried out that the industrial revolution was spawning monsters called corporations. These ruthless business organizations were led by men who had more irresponsible power than any robber baron from the Dark Ages. How, asked Lloyd, could the traditional American ideals of liberty and equality survive the re-creation of feudalism?

The intellectually troubled Howells, financially secure because of the success of his romantic novels of the 1870's, resigned from *The Atlantic* in 1881. He moved to New York, attracted by the vitality of the financial capital of the new industrial empire. Boston was the hub of a universe that no longer existed, the capital of a now vanished ideal. Jeffersonian tranquility had been replaced by the furious growth of a new and dynamic reality—urban and industrial —and its center was New York. Perhaps here he could learn the truth about the new economic environment which so many said was creating two equally corrupted classes—the very rich and the very poor.

He observed the city slums, and considered the criticism of the capitalist system which was said to be responsible for the jungle. From American and English socialists, above all from Tolstoy, he learned that the Jeffersonian dream had been undermined by a capitalist ethic of class warfare and personal selfishness and that there would be no social peace until the gospel of greed and grab was replaced by an ethic of social cooperation and Christian love.

This new outlook was crystallized for Howells by the Haymarket Riot in Chicago on May 5, 1886. He was appalled by the violence of the rioters but even more by the bloody vengeance demanded by respectable citizens. He worked feverishly to check the hysteria directed against the anarchists, yet failed. He had seen the living reality of Mark Twain's lynch mobs that had surged through *The Prince and the Pauper, Huckleberry Finn,* and were soon to fill the pages of *The Connecticut Yankee.* What could be done to keep America from committing itself permanently to this bestiality so reminiscent of feudal Europe and the feudal South? How could one keep America from slipping off the pinnacle of the Jeffersonian covenant with nature back into the abyss of a new dark age?

Obviously Howells's faith of 1865 was shattered, the national faith that each man pursuing his own self-interest would work in harmony with his fellow atoms of selfishness because of the mysterious guiding hand of the natural law of *laissez-faire.* But what was the relation of man to man if the doctrine of *laissez-faire* had proved to be a fallacious myth? After all, Howells, like Twain, had accepted the idea of history as progress and the triumph of liberty for the individual. The climax of historical progress was supposed to have occurred in the Jeffersonian republic when every individual had become autonomous and had achieved harmony with natural law. But this ideal, Howells saw, was not the reality of the 1870's and 1880's. Americans were building a new complexity; they were savagely exploiting one another. There was no peace, no harmony.

Howells's first critical novel of the 1880's marks the beginning of his effort to understand a dynamic reality which he had never learned about from his utopian father. *A Modern Instance* begins in the tranquil and prosaic setting of Equity, Maine, with Bartley Hubbard, editor of the local paper, in love with Marcia Gaylord, daughter of one of the town's prominent lawyers. Here is the backbone of the nation, the middle-class leaders of smalltown America. These citizens of the New World forge their own successful destinies; the stuff they are made of is good and there are no corrupt European social or political institutions or traditions to frustrate the expression of that innate goodness. But the marriage of Bartley and Marcia does not end in happiness forever after; it ends in personal disaster for Bartley and the foundering of the marriage. Why?

Howells's answer is destructive of all the intellectual security of post-Civil War America. Bartley Hubbard is the symbolic hero of that America—the self-made man, free from the restraints of European society. He is the natural man and "the natural man," wrote Howells, "is a wild beast, and his natural goodness is the amiability of a beast basking in the sun." The tragic flaw in Bartley and in Marcia is that they lack a sense of their own limitations; the American social climate fosters the antisocial instincts in man. And the antisocial man is doomed to tragedy. Boundless opportunity and choice—the American creed—is a false philosophy for the individual.

In dramatic contrast to this larger, anarchic American

society, dominated by the democratic and destructive figure of the self-made man, Howells presents the particular society of aristocratic tradition represented by Squire Gaylord, Ben Halleck, and Atherton. It is Atherton who most strongly reminds Ben Halleck that a man is not completely free to follow his impulses. "We're all bound together. No one sins or suffers to himself. . . . Every link in the chain feels the effect of the violence. . . It's the implanted goodness that saves,—the seed of righteousness treasured from generation to generation. . . . the flower of this implanted goodness is what we call civilization." The lesson for Atherton is clear; the elite must act from a sense of moral obligation to the entire society, they must sublimate their individual interests in concern for the general.

Americans were not incorruptible; evil as well as goodness was inherent, and the American gospel of personal success inevitably suppresses the goodness and encourages the evil in the individual and so in the mass. The only hope was in the aristocratic remnant whose traditions of social restraint were stronger than the democratic values of money-making.

In short, Howells saw the impossibility of return to the Jeffersonian dream, just as Twain saw it in *Life on the Mississippi*. But Howells at the beginning of the 1880's, no more than Twain, was ready to surrender the dream of free and equal individuals, transcending the corruption of society to find permanent harmony with nature. And so, just as Twain followed his disastrous confrontation of reality with a nostalgic romance that searched for the ideal of triumphant innocence in *The Prince and the Pauper*, Howells did the same in *The Rise of Silas Lapham*.

He reaffirmed his faith that average Americans, the Silas Laphams, could rise above the morality of tooth and claw. Howells did not completely renounce his belief in the importance of social environment; it provides the structure for our understanding of the democratic Laphams and the aristocratic Coreys. Still, he would reassure his readers that social environment was not everything.

His treatment of the Laphams then is much more sympathetic than it was of Bartley Hubbard, his treatment of the Coreys less sympathetic than it was of Atherton. As Bromfield Corey says, "We represent a faded tradition. We don't really care what business a man is in, so it is large enough, and he doesn't advertise too offensively; but we think it fine to affect reluctance." In contrast, Lapham is a man of innate dignity and worth who is sorely tempted by personal vanity and business opportunity to surrender his native simplicity and honesty, but who makes the right decision and finds personal happiness. Indeed, now that Howells has discovered social environment, his message seems to be that the individual must transcend it. The Laphams may not be able to rise to the level of the Coreys as representatives of a class, nor the Coreys to fall to the level of the Laphams. But, symbolized by the love of a Corey and a Lapham for one another, it is the innate worth and dignity of the individual which is important.

The suggestion is that a new society is possible in America, one which fuses the energy of the new middle class with the manners of the aristocracy without the materialism of the middle class or the artificiality of the aristocracy. Such a society, which connects individuals in terms of personal sympathy and respect, would fulfill the ideal of the Jeffersonian republic. It is perhaps indicative of Howells's nostalgia for a lost paradise that Lapham, after rejecting temptation in the city, retreats to the simpler environment of the country.

From this essay in escape, Howells turns to confront the philosophical dilemma of the 1880's. In two major novels, *Annie Kilburn* and *A Hazard of New Fortunes*, he is moving toward a different definition of his dilemma and, therefore, toward other possible solutions. Apparently he felt that the solution to the loss of the Jeffersonian republic was not the renewed covenant with nature which Twain explored in *Huckleberry Finn* nor the forward thrust of technology considered in *The Connecticut Yankee*. For Howells, the Jeffersonian ideal needed to be redefined to mean equality through brotherly love and cooperation; it must mean social cooperation, rather than the self-sufficient individualism of Huck and the Yankee. The problem was how to transcend the inculcated selfishness of American business culture, how to dissolve the class structure of the new urban-industrial society. What Howells now wanted was a cooperative, classless society of equal brothers to work the factories and to inhabit the cities of late nineteenth-century America. He was no longer primarily concerned with the salvation of the individual, but with the fate of the community.

In *Annie Kilburn,* we are presented with a community tragically divided by stereotyped values which obsure the true needs of the individual. Classless Americans have become proletarians, bourgeois, and aristocrats. They do not see each other as brothers but as aliens and mortal enemies. The businessman, Gerrish, like Bartley Hubbard, is a representative of American business culture but a more articulate one. "I came into this town a poor boy," he explains, "without a penny in my pocket, and I have made my own way, every inch of it, unaided and alone . . . I do not believe in pampering those who have not risen, or have made no effort to rise." Gerrish and his business class cannot view the workers as brothers, or accept them as individuals. To them, such men have failed the test of moral courage.

Annie Kilburn, the aristocratic philanthropist, also sees mankind through a vision dominated by inherited culture; she offers alms not love to the poverty-stricken, alms not justice. She too accepts the inevitability of class lines and poverty. She will give charity to those below her but not the opportunity to climb above their class. How then can the urban-industrial jungle of class exploitation be overcome if American leadership is exhausted by men like Gerrish and women like Annie Kilburn?

The reality of complex society as the inevitable environment for imperfect man is the theme of Howells's masterpiece, the autobiographical novel entitled *A Hazard of New Fortunes*.

Basil March is a Bostonian brought to New York to edit a magazine. He wants to understand the economic basis of this journal and its implications for the relations of the people who are involved in the enterprise. Central in the enterprise is Fulkerson, who has promoted the idea of the magazine, and Dryfoos, who has provided the financial backing. For March, Fulkerson becomes something of an archetype. He is not evil; he is simply the typical American businessman who has no feeling that the economic system is good or bad; he accepts the existence of the profit system and works within it.

Connected with the magazine are Colonel Woodburn from the South and Lindau from Germany. Both react violently against the competitive system of which the magazine is a part; harmony is possible if the emphasis on private property is done away with. Colonel Woodburn speaks for the feudal heritage of the pre-Civil War South where competitive disharmony and exploitation were avoided through paternalism. Lindau is a socialist. Through the centuries, Europeans have looked to the United States as a promised land where they could escape the inequalities of their feudal traditions and institutions. But Lindau has discovered that America had its own feudal lords, the men who own the means of production. Private property has not brought an end to institutional hierarchy and complexity; if the American promise of brotherhood was to be fulfilled, there must be a revolution to destroy the profit system which forces men to exploit one another. For Lindau, the gentle socialist, blood must flow in the streets before the ideal of the American Eden becomes fact.

Basil March shares the German's dream of the meaning of America, but not his faith in violent revolution as the cure for society's ills. Dryfoos, the entrepreneur, is Lindau's symbol of the capitalist as robber baron exploiting his workers. But March refuses to believe that brotherhood can be ushered in by the destruction of Dryfoos. The capitalists were not robber barons who self-consciously set themselves off from the people and constructed a set of laws and institutions to imprison the workers; they were as much prisoners of the system as the men who worked for them.

March comes to see Dryfoos as the symbolic representative of the death of the Jeffersonian republic. Once Dryfoos had farmed in Ohio. But beneath the soil were the natural treasures that were to make possible the building of the urban industrial frontier. Dryfoos, the Jeffersonian, might have been content to live in harmony with the sail but like all men he had "the poison of that ambition to go somewhere," and when chance located natural gas under his farm, he sold out. Now he had nothing to do but to invest his money; he became immensely wealthy. Searching for a business for his son, he met Fulkerson and invested in the magazine. This was Lindau's robber baron, a simple, poorly educated farmer whose family had probably emigrated from Germany several generations earlier.

Dryfoos was so naive that he did not realize ownership of the magazine was different from ownership of the farm. His farm had been a family enterprise but now many men worked for him and although they were dependent on him for their daily bread, he refused to accept responsibility. As far as he was concerned, every man in America still had the opportunity of being economically independent. The magazine was his private property and he would not bargain with his workers about their share of the profits.

March learns to see Dryfoos as a confused, but not an

evil man. He did not want to exploit his workers any more than he had wanted to leave the farm. He is a Jeffersonian attempting to preserve his autonomy and independence on the urban frontier. Completely disillusioned with his new life, frustrated by his inability to control his life and that of his children, he cries out in rage when his wife asks him to return to the country.

"We can't go back! . . . The money don't seem to buy anything but more and more care and trouble. We got a big house that we ain't at home in; and we got a lot of hired girls around under our feet that hinder and don't help. Our children don't mind us, and we got no friends or neighbors. But it had to be. I couldn't help but sell the farm, and we can't go back to it, for it ain't there."

Howells has turned away from the fantasy of Silas Lapham. The Jeffersonian republic no longer exists. The American reality is a complex society of complex individuals. Dryfoos can't understand why his daughter is bewildered by the attentions of a worthless charmer, nor how his son, Conrad, has developed sympathy for the workers. His simple maxims serve neither his children nor himself in the complexity of the new economy and the new society. He does not admit his dependence on the social and economic web until Conrad is killed trying to save Lindau from police brutality.

Conrad's sacrificial death cannot regenerate American society, but it brings a new understanding to his father. Dryfoos, like March, is now aware that he is not self-sufficient; he has learned charity. Like March he comes to understand the interrelationship of society and the necessity of treating each person with dignity.

Was this Howells's final definition of reality? Had he in a sense returned to Hawthorne's vision of the sinful brotherhood of mankind? Was there no hope for the resurrection of the American Adam?

We have explicit evidence that Howells in the 1890's

took an extremely ambivalent attitude toward the future. As a realist, he saw man as a mixture of good and evil, living in a society that shared this dualism; the highest achievement of man was to live by the values of love, responsibility, and charity. One did one's best, like Basil March, to give love and charity, to act responsibly, knowing full well that this best would not eradicate disharmony and evil from the world.

Howells had a strength which Twain lacked. He had purged himself of nostalgia for the Jeffersonian republic. He had found dignity in the acceptance of the new society. He still dreamed of a utopia which might appear out of the urban-industrial frontier, but he would not go mad with Huck when the dream of the Jeffersonian covenant with nature disintegrated. Nor would be believe with the Yankee that industrialism inexorably was leading to tyranny and death. At the beginning of the 1890's, Howells did not try, like Mark Twain, to find saving grace in an historical miracle out of the past. For him, heaven might still exist in the future. And so, abandoning the realism of his novels to indulge in fantasy, he wrote *A Traveler from Altruria*.

In this romance and its sequel, *Through the Eye of the Needle*, Howells indulged himself in an escape from reality, an escape that might be possible if man was corrupted only by external conditions. If Basil March was the spokesman for Howells, the realist, Mr. Homos, the traveler from Altruria, is the spokesman for Howells, the utopian.

Altruria, where men live "for each other" and not "upon each other" as in America, is not a land of primitive simplicity. Howells had no thought of doing away with science, technology, and the arts. His utopia was modern; the Altrurian community centered around great urban cultural complexes with universities, theaters, galleries, museums, laboratories, conservatories, and cathedrals, filled with poets, actors, painters, sculptors, musicians, architects.

This was the smiling side of Howells who proclaimed

in 1895, "It seems to me that we are always mistaking our conditions for our natures, and saying that human nature is greedy and mean and false and cruel, when only its conditions are so." And, in 1896, "The millennium, the reign of Christliness on earth, will be nothing mystical or strange. It will be the application of a very simple rule to life, which we find in no wise difficult or surprising, when the economic conditions do not hinder its operation. The members of a family live for one another as unconsciously as they live upon all others. There is no effort, no friction, in their perpetual surrender of their several interests to the common good; and in the state there need really be none, if once the means of livelihood were assured to each citizen. . . . I believe the right will win in the end." There are the sentiments of his letters and his essays of the nineties, the same sentiments on which his utopian romances were built.

But there was another Howells during this decade, the one who had found corruption in the heart of the American Adam, and who expressed himself in a small volume of poems, *Stops of Various Quills*. Howells, the American innocent, is appalled at the Eternal Adam he finds in men but at last admits that he and every other man are members of Hawthorne's sinful brotherhood.

The novels of the 1880's had culminated in 1890 with Basil March's awareness of the seamless web of society and his responsibility to live within it. Now during the 1890's, even as Howells wrote of escape from historical society in the Altrurian romances and in his letters and essays, these poems reveal that, in his heart, he knew there was to be no millennium because man could not escape his own fallible nature. If Howells was to return to the novel of realism then, he must make the fact of the Eternal Adam central to human experience, must make his characters live within history.

The realistic Howells knew what man's fate was. One could not wait for the millennium. One must act with love and responsibility and charity in the imperfect world of time.

In *The Son of Royal Langbrith,* he asks Americans to confront the existence of evil not as a social problem and not as an individual problem but as men really experienced evil—something which intertwined their public and private lives into a single unit.

In this late novel, Howells preaches the existence of the sinful brotherhood of mankind as the reality of American experience. But, perhaps because he was still so committed to the hope of Mr. Homos and his utopia, he was unable to develop his story of social affirmation as a true work of art. The climax of his skill as a novelist had come with *A Hazard of New Fortunes,* when Basil March had discovered the meaning of the new America. Howells could take an intellectual step beyond March's stance as an observer; he could lecture on the need for responsible action. He could not, however, fuse his heart and his mind. As a work of art *A Son of Royal Langbrith* is contrived and labored. It is only a philosophic tract.

## 3

It was for Howells's other contemporary, Henry James, to so transcend the myth of the American Adam that he could accept history with his heart as well as his mind and express his new commitment in novels that were brilliant artistic achievements.

Unlike Mark Twain and William Dean Howells, Henry James came from an old and established eastern family. It is an indication of the national triumph of the Jacksonian imagination that many of the eastern intellectuals were not only converted to its principles but became its spokesmen. James's father was more of the persuasion of George Bancroft than of Cooper, Hawthorne, and Melville. The younger James was educated by a father committed to his own particular theory of religious millennialism. But when the

young aristocrat measured these ideals against his experience
with the reality of the America of the Civil War era, he
became aware that nothing resembling a restored Garden
existed in the United States. James, like his midwestern
contemporaries, turned to the novel as the means of ex-
ploring the cause of this gap between the ideal of a harmonious New World Eden and the reality of the disorderly
and disharmonious society which covered the land with its
crude imperfections.

Raised with the direct awareness of the Old World
that came from travel in Europe, James focused his searching metaphysical novels on the relationship of Americans
to Europeans. Happily, he had the material resources to confront with his own experience the philosophical assumptions
of the Jacksonian imagination about the differences between
the cultures of the two continents. He was in a position to
question the validity of the persuasion that while the human
condition of tragedy and comedy obtained in Europe, it
had ceased to define man's fate in America. He could test
the assumption that in Europe there was continual frustration for the individual within the confines of an historical
community while the American experienced Edenlike harmony as an autonomous and innocent individual outside of
society.

Although James deserted his native land to take up
permanent residence in old England, his novels are as
American as those of Twain and Howells; they express the
inescapable need of the American novelist to inquire into
the truth of the faith in an American Adam. His self-
imposed exile suggests that he was early disillusioned with
the possibility of the New World Garden. His ceaseless
analysis of the myth of America for the next three decades
also suggests that James could not easily free himself from
the cultural values of his youth. The pattern of his novels
which fill the years from the 1870's into the beginning of
the new century reveals a man whose mind defines the

American Adam as a fraudulent figure but whose heart is at a loss to find a meaning in life to replace that represented by the fallen idol.

As James's analytic intelligence continued to dissect the American situation, to probe its ever deeper levels of hypocrisy and even evil, he began to find values upon which he could build a new life. Ironically, he was to find the source of his rebirth in Europe. He would find the possibility of regeneration in accepting as good the human condition which the Jacksonians had seen embodied in Europe's corrupt historical civilization. Like Hawthorne's Arthur Dimmesdale, Henry James ultimately was to achieve personal salvation through the affirmation of his membership in mankind's sinful brotherhood.

There seems little doubt that when James left the United States he was certain that traditions and institutions were necessary for human existence. The question was whether the individual might achieve dignity from contact with those institutions and traditions. James reversed the epic voyage of his Puritan ancestors. They had sailed away from the Old World convinced that its historical institutions and traditions destroyed human dignity. They had postulated their regeneration in the New World freed from the oppression of social complexity, had believed that innocence was possible when the individual escaped the disharmony imposed upon him by social complexity. Now that James was convinced that the imperfect individual could never achieve innocence, he was impelled to explore the possibility that the Puritans were mistaken in their other premise, that institutions and traditions necessarily destroy human dignity.

His first metaphysical novel, *The American,* was written during 1876-1877, the years that marked the beginning of his permanent exile in England. One is immediately reminded of Cooper's Leatherstocking when one meets Christopher Newman, the American. Here is Natty Bumppo adapted to the business frontier of 1870. Christopher Newman has no parents, no relatives, no friends, no human attachments. Like Deerslayer, he is also "a self-reliant young man who does seem to have sprung from nowhere and whose characteristic pose . . . was the solitary stance in the presence of nature and God." This is the American Adam as "the hero in space" who "seems to take his start outside time."

Christopher Newman is self-reliant, but not self-sufficient. Here James's allegory diverges from that of Cooper, who had written the history of a myth that could not find human fulfillment. James relates the history of a man who could not find fulfillment in the values of the Adamic myth. Newman has made his fortune in the West, but he has done so at the price of spiritual bankruptcy and social sterility. Complacent, he does not understand he is traveling back to Europe because there is nothing to sustain life in the West. But blinded to his essential humanity by his self-image of innocence and perfection, he will fail to become part of the human community which Europe represents. He may hope to possess Europe's treasures but cannot participate in its society. He wants to find "the biggest kind of entertainment a man can get. People, places, art, nature, everything! I want to see the tallest mountains, and the bluest lakes, and the finest pictures, and the handsomest churches, and the most celebrated men, and the most beautiful women."

James establishes a devastating contrast between the American's definition of common sense, as spiritual autonomy and material success, with the experience of civilization that such a philosophy of selfish pride must always lead to a comic or a tragic fall. Christopher Newman believes he is a completely free individual. For James, however, the American is a prisoner of the most extreme metaphysical delusions. His common-sense experience of material things has no relation to the life of man in society.

In *The Pathfinder*, Cooper built his allegorical drama around the need of Leatherstocking for a wife, but the myth could not consummate a fruitful relationship with a flesh and blood woman. If Christopher Newman remains the prisoner of the myth which cuts him off from an appreciation of the human condition, he too will be unable to make a marriage in reality.

James's violent attack on the American appears to us in subtle form because Newman is the interpreter of his own confrontation with historical society. George Bancroft could not have imagined a more melodramatic contest than that of this Jacksonian American knight against the reactionary forces of medieval darkness, the de Bellegardes. Newman has met a charming and cultivated young widow, Madame de Centre, a member of the de Bellegarde family. He has decided that he will rescue her from meaningless existence and marry her passive cultivation to his active virility. He is St. George rescuing a fair damsel in distress from her dragon-like family, imprisoned in the medieval past.

He has no doubt that Madame de Centre will marry him. Why should she not prefer his perfect innocence and overwhelming affluence to the corruption and poverty of her family, who certainly must see the advantage of a rich son-in-law? Even if they choose to cling to the artificial values of the past, they can understand the expediency of this fresh infusion of wealth that will allow them to live by their outmoded and non-productive standards. All the problems of family ties and beliefs must vanish before the force of his frontier autonomy and his money.

" 'It is my mother's wish, and mine, that no such allusions should be made,' the Marquis de Bellegarde tells him. 'Pray never make them yourself. We prefer to assume that the person accepted as the possible husband of my sister is one of ourselves, and that he should have no explanations to make. With a little discretion on both sides, everything, I think, will be easy. This is exactly what I wished to say— that we quite understand what we have undertaken, and that you may depend upon our adhering to our resolution. . . . I am sure you understand me.'

" 'Oh no, I don't understand you at all,' said Newman. 'But you needn't mind that, I don't care. In fact, I think I had better not understand you. I might not like it. That wouldn't suit me at all, you know!' "

Faced with Newman's refusal to compromise his autonomy and become a member of the family, the de Bellegardes reject his suit, and Claire de Centre breaks off her engagement. Newman retreats to America, horrified at the evil that European institutions and traditions can impose upon the individual. He, himself, has retained his independence and innocence, and he returns to the West as prideful, as blind to the human condition, as when he left. He cannot conceive that Madame de Centre has denied his power to provide her with perfection outside of historical society, and has sought salvation elsewhere.

James allows his American to write the script of a Jacksonian melodrama and then asks his fellow countrymen if they are still able to see this American as representing absolute good or Europeans absolute evil. Was the American Adam really the unambiguous hero that Newman proclaimed himself? The irony of this approach becomes still more pointed when, in his next novel, James makes the American his heroine.

In *The Portrait of a Lady*, Isabel Archer comes to Europe the same kind of orphan hero as Christopher Newman. Like him, she cannot sustain herself as a self-sufficient atom of self-interest. Instinctively, she too needs the richness, the variety of society to fulfill her potential as a human being. Like Newman, she believes that she can buy the richness and variety of Europe without compromising her autonomous innocence, without committing herself to the society which had produced the treasures she wants.

Isabel Archer is the "unbounded" American who has the power of "total possibility." "She was always planning out her development, desiring her perfection, observing her progress. . . . She had an unquenchable desire to think well of herself. . . . She had a theory that it was only under this provision that life was worth living; that one should be one of the best, should be conscious of a fine organization (she couldn't help knowing her organization was fine), should move in a realm of light, of natural wisdom, of happy impulse, of inspiration gracefully chronic. . . . She spent half her time in thinking of beauty and bravery and magnanimity; she had a fixed determination to regard the world as a place of brightness, of free expansion, of irresistible action; she held it must be detestable to be afraid or ashamed. She had an infinite hope that she should never do anything wrong."

Although it is plain that James is describing Isabel Archer in the radiant terms of her own self-image, some critics have been outraged that the author should allow this freedom-loving dove to become imprisoned in the gilded cage of Gilbert Osmond. But James has not described a freedom-loving dove. He has presented us with an American innocent who is as much the prisoner of her own ideology as was Christopher Newman. Because she refuses to compromise her metaphysical ideals in the face of human experience, she is incapable of creative or constructive activity.

Isabel must marry Osmond precisely because she does not understand the advice of Madame Merle that she should make a marriage which will provide a suitable material context for her soul. Human dignity, Madame Merle informs Isabel, depends upon a healthy social environment. Isabel, however, will not listen to Madame Merle because, for the American girl, this European woman's nature "has been too much overlaid by custom and her angles too much rubbed away. She had become too flexible, too useful, was too ripe and too final. . . . Isabel found it difficult to think of her in any detachment or privacy. She existed only in her relations, direct or indirect, with her fellow mortals."

Isabel, in her American pride, refuses to admit her dependence upon "her fellow mortals." She has refused the suit of the real European, Lord Warburton, because this young English peer represented the living reality of Old World traditions and institutions and she feared being drawn "into the system in which he . . . lived and moved."

Gilbert Osmond is the perfect husband for her. He is an American who likes European things and collects European art, but feels no commitment to European traditions and institutions. Like Gilbert, Isabel wants the details of Europe for external exhibition, but permits no deeper relation for fear of endangering her autonomous soul. And just as there was no possible happy ending for Christopher Newman, the American, who refused to compromise his self-sufficiency, so Isabel Archer is doomed to a stoic continuation of her meaningless marriage. "I can't change that way . . . one must accept one's deeds. I married him before all the world; I was perfectly free; it was impossible to do anything more deliberate. One can't change that way."

Isabel and her fellow Americans will never be free and responsible until they reject the ideology which insists that all goodness is within the individual and all evil within society. Indeed, James has reached the implicit position that the worst evil which exists in the world is the result of the excessive pride of the individual. One can begin to see that Christopher Newman and Isabel Archer are the children of Roger Chillingworth and Captain Ahab. In the name of their own inner perfection, they leave the world worse than they found it.

James had dissolved the dualism by which the Jacksonian imagination divided civilization between Old World evil and New World goodness, between an unfree society and the free individual; this dualism no longer defined the reality of existence. The American, in the pride of his self-image as a creature of common sense, had proved to be cut off from common sense, from an appreciation of the reality of the human condition. Living in a world of ideology, he was divorced from human experience. To understand him,

James sought to probe the roots of this ideology of the American Adam.

Cooper, Hawthorne, and Melville might have told him to look back to the philosophy of the French Revolution to see the American democrat as the intellectual heir of Jean Jacques Rousseau. But James was raised within the Jacksonian establishment, and the Jacksonians insisted that they had learned of liberty, equality, and fraternity from their experience with the West. They claimed that as the children of nature they owed nothing to European theory, and even denied the existence of any ideology as the basis of New World democracy. Democracy, the freedom of the individual from all traditions and institutions, was intrinsic to the frontier condition.

James had to rediscover the revolutionary ground upon which the American imagination was based. Living in England during the second half of the nineteenth century, he found an analogy in the anarchists of Europe. Ostensibly, *The Princess Casamassima* has nothing to do with the United States at all, but there is devastating irony in relating Hyacinth Robinson, the hero of this novel, to the tradition of the heroic American orphan of the natural wilderness.

Hyacinth is the child of a French prostitute, perhaps fathered by a drunken English aristocrat, and raised by a London seamstress; he is the offspring of the social wilderness. His foster mother raises him to believe in his noble parentage so that Hyacinth, like the American Adam, is outside of society; he is alienated from the lower class without being part of the aristocracy. Using this European as hero, James drives home his point that no one can transcend society except through an ideology that blinds the individual to the reality of institutions and traditions.

Hyacinth Robinson, the self-sufficient, self-reliant, autonomous man, follows the path of Christopher Newman and

Isabel Archer. He cannot live in isolation, he is attracted by culture, but he despises the aristocracy which governs society. If there is to be social justice, the structure of the community must be smashed. The traditions and institutions which justify inequality must be destroyed in the name of freedom.

As Hyacinth labors at the art of bookbinding, however, he discovers that he no longer considers he is being exploited by the social establishment. He is an artist and the fulfillment of his love of beauty and his craftmanship is made possible by the existence of hierarchical, historical institutions and traditions. He comes to see that if a revolution in the name of anarchy succeeds, then the great treasures of the past will be destroyed and the opportunity to participate in the creation of new beauty will be lost.

When he has reached the point of fearing mediocrity more than he hates inequality, he comes under the spell of the Princess Casamassima, who persuades him to join her anarchist conspiracy. Civilization must be destroyed in order to liberate the people and bring about social justice. The princess exists for the cause; she has no feeling for Hyacinth as a human being. Just as Hawthorne and Melville had dramatized the alienation, the ideological madness of Chillingworth and Ahab by setting them apart from and against humanity, so James's princess has no social roots, no place in the community. To bring into existence an impossible vision of human perfection she is ready to exploit Hyacinth or anyone else to try to impose this dream upon mankind.

So begins Hyacinth Robinson's final education in the meaning of reality. The conspiratorial cell he joins is committed to the ideal of human freedom from all institutional restraint. The members argue, like Christopher Newman and Isabel Archer, that society necessarily destroys human dignity. But what does human dignity mean for the Princess and her fellow conspirators? It is abstract freedom for another abstraction—the people. They obey only a cold, in-

human, and logical cause. Hyacinth discovers that while rebellion was possible within society, it is impossible within
this band of saints. There is no escape from the rigid restrictions which their ideology of total freedom places upon its
adherents. Death is his only means to transcend this most
absolute of all prisons.

He is redeemed in death, however, by his final vision
of the good. He has seen that the good will not be found in
the alienation of the individual from the community. Man's
only meaningful freedom is achieved in his participation in
the great treasure of infinite variety which is the heritage of
tradition. It is to be found in the acceptance of social life
in its concrete diversity. This is a freedom that demands
love and responsibility.

Christopher Newman had learned almost nothing from
his initiation into the human condition and had retreated
back into the emptiness and sterility of the American myth.
Isabel Archer was almost as superficial as Newman in her
approach to the significance of human relations. Now
Hyacinth Robinson had reached a level of perception of
social reality that was esthetic as well as intellectual. He
was learning to become a true member of society when the
chains of his earlier ideological commitment dragged him
to his death.

If these books reveal the pilgrim's progress of Henry
James as he retraced the philosophical steps that had led
his Puritan ancestors away from European civilization to
the western wilderness, then we should be prepared to
expect a novel which would summarize his discoveries, his
education in the human condition as it existed in Europe,
and the ideological barbarism that prevailed in America.
There is no more symbolic title for a history of his pilgrimage
than *The Ambassadors,* which is indeed an essay in oblique
autobiography as James relates the story of a middle-aged
American gentleman who takes a first and hesitant step toward an acceptance of Europe with love.

*The Ambassadors* begins as if it is to be a sequel to
*The American*, with only a minor modification of the traditional Jacksonian melodrama. Chad Newsome, upstanding
and innocent young American, has traveled to Paris. There,
it is feared, he has been seduced by a woman of the world,
Madame de Vionnet. His mother, a simple and good American widow and upholder of American virtue, acts to rescue
her son from this creature of the depths. Her champion will
be Lambert Strether, sober and responsible American businessman and platonic friend, who will sally forth from the
American Eden in Woollett, Massachusetts, travel into the
land of corruption, France, penetrate the citadel of evil, Paris,
and rescue the fair young man from the wicked queen of
darkness. At fifty-five Strether is still a child who has not
yet been initiated into reality, an infant who has always
accepted the authority of the American woman, represented
by Mrs. Newsome. He believes that the American woman,
unlike her European counterpart, is absolutely and im-
mutably pure.

When he finds Madame de Vionnet so exquisite, so
charming, so civilized, he rejects the possibility that she is
capable of sin. It seems to him that Chad Newsome is richer
intellectually and culturally for his association with this
woman. He is convinced that the two are enjoying only a
platonic and intellectual relationship. But then he discovers
them together at an inn outside of Paris. Can Mrs. Newsome
be right after all? Yet Strether cannot help being impressed
by Madame de Vionnet's poise. She continues to act as if she
and Chad were on an innocent picnic. What hypocrisy, he
cries inwardly, but then how well her manners have kept
life from disintegrating into unbearable crisis. Strether re-
flects that people sin in America, even though they deny the
possibility of sin. In France, the possibility is accepted and
people have developed the technique of living with it.

Madame de Vionnet, he sees, is at the same time both
a sinful and a generous woman. In her relationship with

Chad, it is she who gives and he who takes. When he tired of her, Chad would return to Woollett and the upright career that awaited him there. It was Chad who was the sinful and selfish member of this affair.

Lambert Strether had reached the last step in his intellectual and spiritual pilgrimage away from Woollett and its evil enchantment. It remained for him only to achieve independence of judgment. If Chad was sinful, it was not because he was seduced by Madame de Vionnet; he had sinned because of his own will. And if this was true, then there was no American Adam, since Americans claimed that sin was caused by traditions and institutions, that the individual in a state of nature would be perfect. The American Adam was a figment of a cultural imagination, not a fact of experience. The American was not free from culture and tradition any more than he was free from sin.

Strether had edited a magazine in Woollett, which received financial support from Mrs. Newsome. He had done her bidding. And yet he had thought of himself as an independent individual, responsible only to himself. This, he saw now, this self-deception, was an indication of the moral inferiority of American culture. The Europeans, accepting the inevitability of human interdependence, were capable of moral responsibility. But Americans denied the dependence of one individual upon another, and this encouraged them to ignore their responsibility for others. Chad Newsome felt he had no responsibility toward Madame de Vionnet. His relationship to her was one of calculated exploitation. And this relationship became even more monstrous when it was placed within the American context of self-righteousness. All of Woollett would gloat at Chad's escape; they would applaud the tragedy of Madame de Vionnet as her just desert because she was a sinful European and he was an innocent American.

America could be viewed as a greatly magnified anarchist cell. In the name of individual freedom, there had been created in the New World a community held together not by human experience, by traditions, or institutions, but by ideology. And every American was the prisoner of this totalitarian metaphysics that forced the individual to be free from love for his neighbor. Strether, however, has escaped the evil enchantment of American cultural conditioning. He can love Madame de Vionnet and have compassion for her tragedy. He can tell Chad, "You'll be a brute, you know—you'll be guilty of the last infamy—if you ever forsake her."

In *The Wings of the Dove*, which followed *The Ambassadors*, James paused in his pursuit of realism to turn back for a final reconsideration of the theme of innocence. It is instructive that James alone at this point can use a traditional American symbol, the young virgin, to express New World innocence. In the figure of Milly Theale, he evokes the myth in its most beautiful transcendence. It is James, not Twain or Howells, who at the end of the 1890's can re-create such an American innocent from the past because he alone has the will and the strength to kill this angel, to bury the memory of America as heaven on earth, and to move on to affirm the worth of European values or rather the values of the human condition. When Milly Theale dies, James at last will be free to give his heart to history.

*The Wings of the Dove* begins with the story of Kate Croy, an English girl. To understand her, one must remember that James shares the philosophy of Madame Merle of *Portrait of a Lady*, who denied Isabel Archer's affirmation that the soul was invulnerable to the influence of the circumstances of life. For Madame Merle, personality could be made beautiful or ugly, depending upon its surroundings. She believes that the virtues of honesty and decency flowered only in a congenial atmosphere. As she told Osmond, "I don't believe at all that it's [the soul is] an immortal principle. I believe it can perfectly be destroyed.

That is what has happened to mine, which was a very good one to start with."

Kate Croy had a very good soul to begin with. She is raised to believe herself a part of the genteel world of the Victorian middle-class aristocracy. But her widowed father is a ne'er-do-well who must live a life of shabby pretense. His resources are so limited that to give his daughter the surroundings of gentility, he must send her to live as the companion of an aristocratic and demanding aunt. Love must be sacrificed to material appearances.

Here lies the tragedy of Kate Croy, she is tough, pragmatic, realistic. She knows that the mundane details of experience are important to the good life, and she is willing to sacrifice her soul to acquire these material necessities. She is in love with a penniless young man, but she refused to marry him until they have wealth; she will not follow her father in a life of desperate pretense. Into this impasse enters Milly Theale from America. If Kate is the tragic orphan of the human condition, Milly is the invincible and invulnerable orphan of the American Eden.

While Kate fights for security against the hostility of a cold and impersonal society, Milly Theale is rich beyond the need of material security. But she feels incomplete without the experience of the world, which she is sure can only be that of beauty and love and which, since it is unavailable in America, can be bought in Europe. She falls in love with Densher, Kate's secret fiancé. Discovering that Milly is dying of an incurable disease, Kate encourages Densher to court Milly and inherit her millions. This would finally enable them to live together in the material circumstances their genteel station in life demands.

In the second half of the novel, the scene shifts to Venice, the city of medieval beauty, a symbolic island of dreams in the sea of harsh reality. Here Milly can play the role of the storied princess of legend, living in an enchanted

castle surrounded by loyal servants, with Densher to seek
her hand in a properly oblique and lengthy suit. James has
taken the dream of total possibility which had possessed
Christopher Newman and Isabel Archer to its farthest extreme. The dream has its last refuge in the feeble body of
Milly Theale in the most isolated and romantic city in
western civilization, and it can exist only as long as Milly
does. The tragic tautology is complete because Milly can
live only as long as she has the dream. Sooner or later, she
must face reality. When Lord Mark tells her that Densher
and Kate have planned to be married, she "turns her face
to the wall." The American dream of total possibility cannot survive the truth of worldly imperfection.

The dying Milly does not know that her love was
winning Densher away from Kate, and that Densher will
reject her fortune and choose to live with her memory. She
does not know that love can have an effect on human relationships. For Milly, the American, love must exist in
transcendence above the web of imperfect social relations
spun by fallible men and women.

James is now ready to bring the melodrama of American separation from Europe to its conclusion. In his last
great novel, *The Golden Bowl,* the American as metaphysical
abstraction will disappear and be replaced by a human
figure who is a member of the sinful brotherhood of mankind.

Adam Verver, a wealthy American who dreams of
building a utopian city in his native land, is in Europe buying art for his museum. A widower, he is accompanied by
his only daughter, Maggie. Between them, there exists a
perfect love. Together, they are self-sufficient and self-
satisfied, and for them, the world is one of total possibility.
They will buy what they want in Europe; they will build
what they want in America.

Like all of James's Americans, they are dependent upon
Europe for the art and the society which they instinctively

need. They, too, in their supposed innocence, have arrived to exploit the artistic and human treasures of the Old World. Adam and Maggie Verver are innocent only if that term is defined as meaning smug, selfish, and irresponsible. Like Christopher Newman and Isabel Archer, even Milly Theale, they want to take everything and give nothing. As Americans, they must act outside of social commitment in order to preserve the perfection of their souls. But, for James, such self-righteous greed can only destroy their souls.

It is decided that Maggie would look well with a cultured Italian, Prince Amerigo, as a decorative husband, and Adam buys him for his daughter. The prince will be a possession of the family, not a member of it. But Maggie comes to feel uneasy about this triangle; she believes it would look more proper if her father were to marry. And so it is decided that a young, impoverished American expatriate, Charlotte Swant, who had acquired the manners and culture of Europe, is the most convenient person to provide balance to the family. Now Adam, like Maggie, has acquired a decorative companion. Since Charlotte is also bought, it is assumed that she too will understand the nature of the marriage and will not disrupt the inhuman companionship of the father and daughter.

There is marvelous irony when James brings Prince Amerigo and Adam Verver into direct familial confrontation as rivals for Maggie. James has long made it clear that the American Adam does not exist in human experience, but is the creation of ideology. What is the source of this ideology? Logically, it must be in Europe because Europeans crossed the Atlantic and declared that in the New World there would be new men—innocent men. If Adam Verver believes that Prince Amerigo is a man of historical experience, Amerigo in turn believes Adam to be a man of natural innocence. The prince believes in the possibility of the kind of marriage which Adam and Maggie want because, for him, they are Americans, they are innocents. And he, the European discoverer of America, accepts an ideological abstraction as an existent reality. When the prince and Charlotte are thrown together in the family and it is revealed that in the past they have been lovers, what is more inevitable than that they should resume the relationship? And what is more inevitable than that they should be certain that Adam and Maggie, living together in the platonic and innocent love of father and daughter, should be incapable of discovering the illicit sexual love within their own home?

When Maggie purchases a golden bowl as a present for her husband, she discovers that Charlotte has considered buying it for her lover. She realizes who that lover must be. When the bowl breaks along its inherent flaw, the flaw which had caused the prince to advise Charlotte against its purchase, she holds it together in her hands. She has the will to preserve her marriage.

If the golden bowl is accepted as a symbol of society, then we are aware of how different is Maggie's commitment to her marriage than was Isabel Archer's. Isabel acts out of pride in her own integrity; she will live with a man whom she does not love in order to sustain her invulnerability in a hostile world. The preservation of her marriage means the preservation of her innocence. When Maggie acts to save her marriage, however, it is because she realizes that she needs the earthly and imperfect love of her husband, not the platonic and perfect love of her father.

In the transformation of Maggie, one is reminded of the experience of Pearl in *The Scarlet Letter*. Pearl strenuously rejected the idea that she had a heavenly, a platonic father. She demanded a father who was a man of this world. And she discovered him in the crisis on the scaffold, that "scene of grief" which "developed all her sympathies" and which promised "that she would grow up amid human joy and sorrow, nor forever do battle with the world, but be a woman in it." Maggie has accepted the grief of her husband's unfaithfulness. She has "developed all her sympathies." From this moment on, she would live "amid human joy and sorrow" and "be a woman in it."

Maggie accepts her guilt. She recognizes that she has not been a wife to Amerigo and that she was responsible for creating a situation that drove him back into the arms of Charlotte. It was her selfishness and that of her father which created the context for wrongdoing. Evil had sprung directly out of their pretended innocence. Marriage, the ultimate unit of community, demanded love and responsibility, and she had given neither. Now she was ready to act with love and responsibility as a member of society.

Responsibility meant that the institutions of society should be preserved, the golden bowl held together. She must win back her husband without creating a crisis between Charlotte and Adam Verver. She becomes a "mistress of shades" as she manipulates the social situation with skill and sophistication. She has accepted fully Madame Merle's council to Isabel Archer that the self is determined by the context in which it exists and that dignity depends upon social relationships.

The author's final, ironic advice to his compatriots is that to achieve freedom, they must surrender independence. This is no paradox for James, however, because he sees American independence as an illusion born of an ideology which denied the fallible and social nature of man. Independence, for Americans, meant innocence. It meant freedom from sin and society. Bound by that ideology, the American was not able to act creatively in the world of experience, the world of sin and society.

Because self-sufficiency was an illusion, the American who was a prisoner of the dream was doomed to experience the only total human tragedy—sterility. That was the fate of Christopher Newman, Isabel Archer, and Milly Theale. To escape from the prison of ideology, Americans must break down the melodramatic dualism of America and Europe. They must proclaim their common humanity which had

always existed beneath the illusion of innocence. Like
Maggie Verver, they must break through the facade of
ideology to find the real self, the social and sinful self, and
reveal to Europe that the American proudly wears
Hawthorne's Scarlet Letter.

# III

---

# THE NATURALISTS

---

*Frank Norris*
*Stephen Crane*
*Theodore Dreiser*

There was no direct communication between the first two generations of American novelists. Conditioned to believe that the ideal of the American Eden was the substance of the national experience, Twain, Howells, and James had had to discover for themselves the difference between myth and reality, between their youthful ideal of the Jeffersonian arcadia and the reality of the post-Civil War urban-industrial society. Ultimately, they came to share the conclusion of Cooper, Hawthorne, and Melville that the human condition continued to prevail in the New World as in the Old, there was no American Eden and no American Adam.

A far more profound intellectual chasm separates these realists from the next generation of American novelists, the naturalists. Frank Norris, Stephen Crane, and Theodore Dreiser reached intellectual maturity within the late nineteenth-century climate of opinion which still held that the most significant experience of the individual in America was to live in accordance with natural law. But the natural law was no longer that of the Enlightenment which had promised that the lion would lie down with the lamb in the New World Eden. Now in the 1870's and 1880's, nature was seen as an evolutionary process and nature's law the survival of the fittest. Once again the American state of nature was defined in terms of European ideology, this time Darwin's theory of evolution.

When the European middle class of the late eighteenth century developed the idea of progress, in which history was viewed as the story of liberty proceeding from the tyranny of the medieval community to the freedom of the autonomous individual in a state of nature, its philosophers attempted to provide a scientific foundation for this millennial dream by appealing to the authority of the physics of Sir Isaac Newton. Mankind, the *philosophes* argued, could escape irrational traditions and institutions, which were always subject to change, by achieving harmony with the laws of nature, which were rational in their eternal and immutable perfection.

While Europeans looked to America as the first home for such a natural utopia, they also believed that, with the American and French Revolutions, the last major vestiges of medieval civilization had begun to crumble everywhere. By 1830, the intellectuals of England, France, and Germany were declaring the freedom of the bourgeoisie from outworn historical traditions and institutions, to live by the rationality of natural law. Just as the triumph of Jacksonian democracy was held to mark a fundamental change in the human condition in the New World, the reform movements in England in the 1830's and 1840's, and the revolutions during those decades in France and Germany, were seen as the culmination of progress toward liberty in the Old World.

European philosophers were then faced with the task of explaining why, with the end of medieval civilization, harmony did not become the modern way of life. England found the answer which most appealed to Americans as they, too, came to recognize that the United States failed to live up to the Newtonian concept of nature.

During the first half of the nineteenth century, English social philosophers and economists presented a new view of nature as dynamic, not static; evolutionary, not immutable. They argued that God had provided such a continuing on-ward and upward thrust of nature because He recognized that man was not yet spiritually perfect. Malthus, Ricardo, and Herbert Spencer pointed out that the eighteenth-century prophets of progress had been wrong in believing that all of the inadequacies of man were imposed upon him by false traditions and institutions. The Enlightenment thinkers had been far too optimistic in believing that man was ready to be a new and redeemed Adam who could now live in eternal harmony in a heavenly city on earth. The truth was that im-perfect humanity, freed from the irrelevancies of historical society, still needed to undergo an extended spiritual catharsis through the beneficent forces of nature that would gradually bring mankind to worldly perfection.

This meant, according to the new spokesmen of pro-gress, the classical economists, that the disharmony of the nineteenth century was to be radically different from that of any previous century. Historical disharmony had been corrupting. Hitherto man had wandered in a wilderness of meaningless institutions and traditions, but now, having escaped from the irrelevancies of man-made law, he could live with the redemptive disharmony of the great natural law of evolution. They saw evolution as operating according to the mechanism of competition, of survival of the fittest, and thus justifying the way of competitive capitalist society. Slowly, evolution would force men to progress upwards, always weeding out the unfit, until finally there would be a saving remnant, a residue of cleansed and purified people who would be deserving of citizenship in a heavenly city on earth.

The American people after 1865 accepted this doctrine of Social Darwinism even more enthusiastically than did England. It allowed them to preserve their national image of being that community which was closest to nature and had progressed farthest from the depths of the Dark Ages. The English social philosophers, like Herbert Spencer, who were prophets with honor in the United States, argued that men must be free from historical culture before they could experience the progressive upward thrust of evolutionary nature. Everyone knew that only in America were there no vestiges of feudal society. Americans could continue to see themselves as a chosen people, closer to nature, closer to God than the peoples of the Old World. Surely it would be Americans who would be redeemed first by evolution.

American popular culture thus found good reason to continue its neglect of Cooper, Hawthorne, and Melville. It could reject the darker theories of Twain and accept the smugness of *The Innocents Abroad,* the nostalgia and the pride in progress of *Life on the Mississippi,* the warmth of *Tom Sawyer,* the triumphant virtue of *The Prince and the Pauper.* It managed also to find only the smiling aspects of William Dean Howells. As for Henry James, all could rejoice that he had taken his un-American ideas into voluntary exile abroad.

This then was the intellectual world in which Crane, Norris, and Dreiser reached maturity. Innocence was not lost, only postponed. Disharmony was not the result of a growing cultural complexity that doomed the covenant with nature. American disharmony only demonstrated the continued existence of that covenant. One could almost say that the greater the disharmony, the more moral and virtuous the community. The young novelists of 1890 did not follow the leadership of Twain, Howells, and James; realism, the discovery of the conflict between the Jeffersonian ideal and the existence of a complex society, had no meaning for them. They were naturalists. The drama of their novels would find its focus in the way in which they accommodated these two theories of nature, the static and peaceful concept of the eighteenth century and that of dynamic conflict put forward in the nineteenth.

# 1

Frank Norris was the only naturalist who came to accept unequivocally this major revision of the national faith. And even he had difficulty in abandoning the Jacksonian persuasion of an already fulfilled innocence within the paradisiacal American Garden. Reluctantly at first but then with mounting enthusiasm, he accepted the Spencerian philosophy of progress that postulated the need for man's further tutelage under the guidance of an evolutionary nature which lifted mankind ever upward through the mechanism of tooth-and-claw competition. During the 1870's and 1880's as he grew to manhood, the only alternative to Herbert Spencer's grim optimism seemed to be the despair of Mark Twain. By 1890, the frontier was gone; the virgin land had been overwhelmed by cities and factories. One must either believe that the disharmony of this new complexity pointed backward to the medieval past or that it was the necessary corollary to progressive evolution through competition.

The young Norris began his writing career tormented by the recognition of the existence of evil. His novels form a pattern which reveals his sustained effort to move from the shock of acceptance of man's continued imperfection to the optimistic outlook that finally this inner weakness was to be transcended through the benevolent, if harsh, influence of evolutionary nature.

In his first two novels, *Vandover and the Brute* and *McTeague*, Norris seems to be asking whether one could properly continue to talk about innocence at all if man was indeed cursed by hereditary evil. For this child of American

Victorian culture, the specific evil which most haunted him was sex. Mark Twain's Jeffersonian republic, built on the redemptive foundation of virgin land, was the home only of mothers and children. But the dream of the Jacksonians of timeless perfection had now been shattered. Mankind did not live in immutable and platonic stasis; men and women begat children who symbolized timeful change. By 1890, American writers could not escape the existence of sex as the biographical basis of the ever-changing historical community.

Vandover was a child of the golden West and of the respectable middle class. But he was motherless. And here we already have the warning that he may not grow up to be a normal American boy since, for the Victorian reader, he is deprived of the stabilizing and purifying influence of a mother. His father had only one interest, his work. Vandover, therefore, reaches adolescence without the moral uplift of a family; he had no moral discipline when "the innate vice stirred in him, the brute began to make itself felt."

Temporarily, the youngster is saved from becoming the slave of his animal appetite. He has a strong, artistic transcendent instinct which leads him to idealize the true, the good, and the beautiful. But his adolescent confusion is compounded when he goes away to college where his dissolute companions encourage him to drink, to gamble, and ultimately to consort with a prostitute.

It is with a profound sense of shame and guilt that he returns to the West resolved to live only at the high level of the spirit and never again to fall victim to lust. But Vandover is unstable. He has not learned the virtue from the mother he never had, or discipline from his father. The prey of his biological impulses, he associates with women of easy virtue who "appealed only to the animal and beast in him, the evil, hideous brute that made instant answer."

Vandover, like all men, is the battleground of good and evil impulses. Which of these is to govern his life? Vandover makes the wrong choice—and for Norris, Vandover was free to choose. "It was the wilful and deliberate corruption of part of that which was best in him." He allows the brute to feed "its abominable hunger from that part of him which he knew to be the purest, the cleanest, and the best."

Choosing this course of corruption, he seduces an innocent girl, who commits suicide when she discovers she is pregnant. Appalled, he runs away, as much from himself as from the scene of his crime. But flight is no escape from his inner problem, and he returns to find his father a victim of suicide brought on by his son's crime. Vandover cannot face his conscience and once more tries to escape in a year of frantic dissolution.

Each day the brute in him destroys another segment of his conscience until it becomes almost all powerful. And yet one day, when Vandover wanders into the opera: "There came over him a vague sense of those things which are too beautiful to be comprehended . . . to be better, to be true and right and pure, these were the only things that were worthwhile. . . . The appeal had been made directly to what was best and strongest in Vandover, and the answer was quick and overpowering. . . . He had not yet destroyed all that was good in him."

But it is too late. When he tries to climb out of the gutter and to re-create the artistic talent which had been his strongest source of spirituality, he finds "It was gone—his art was gone, the one thing that could save him. That, too, like all the other good things of his life he had destroyed." The brute has established its permanent superiority, and Vandover is its prisoner.

For Norris the story of Vandover was tragic because his hero had free will but made the wrong choice and, therefore, "his whole life had been one long suicide." The possibility of innocence still remained for men, even though they were burdened by inherited evil and bound to the wheel of ongoing evolution. It was the chance circumstance of Vandover's broken family which had swung the balance toward tragedy.

For Norris, chance, not biological determinism, played the crucial role in swinging the balance of an individual's life between his inherent goodness and his inherent evil. He was to affirm this conclusion even more emphatically in his next novel, *McTeague*. It is odd how consistently critics have made biological determinism the central theme of this book. Perhaps they have been misled because they have not taken into account the Victorian values of class difference which were such an important part of the author's artistic imagination. For the critics, McTeague has less free will than Vandover, but, for Norris, McTeague's situation is the result of his lower class status and not his greater vulnerability to domination by physical law. Lower-class status indicated less intelligence as well as less education.

McTeague had become a dentist by chance, and it is chance that brings Trina, an attractive, uneducated girl, into his office. Now "This poor crude dentist of Polk Street, stupid, ignorant, vulgar, with his sham education and plebian tastes, whose only relaxations were to eat, to drink steam beer, to play upon his concertina, was living through his first romance, his first idyll."

Filled with lust, "McTeague fought against it, moved by an unreasoned instinct of resistance. Within him, a certain second self, another better McTeague rose with the brute; both were strong, with the huge crude strength of the man himself. . . . There in that cheap and shabby 'Dental Parlor' a dreaded struggle began. It was the old battle, old as the world, wide as the world—the sudden panther leap of the animal . . . and the simultaneous arousing of the other man, the better self . . . Below the fine fabric of all that was good in him ran the foul stream of hereditary evil, like a sewer. The vices and sins of his father and father's father, to the third and fourth and five hundredth generation, tainted, the evil of an entire race flowed in his veins."

It was chance that tipped the scale. Presumably if McTeague had fallen in love with a girl who could have strengthened his spiritual instincts, his life might have been different. But in Trina's case as in McTeague's it was a matter of brute responding to brute. Another man might have aroused the higher instincts of Trina who now as she looked at McTeague felt "the second self that had wakened in her, and that shouted and clamored for recognition."

And so McTeague and Trina get married, and "Their undoing was already begun. Yet neither of them was to blame. . . . Chance had brought them face to face. . . . Neither of them had asked that this thing should be—that their destinies, their very souls, should be the sport of chance. If they could have known, they would have shunned the fearful risk. But they were allowed no choice in the matter."

Even as we watch Trina and McTeague disintegrate into total bestiality, we are aware of Norris's refutation of the meaningless determinism of man by natural law. For Norris, God was still benevolent, nature was fruitful, and man would be redeemed. He had questioned the new national faith and found it correct in its essential affirmations. The hereditary weakness in man was not all powerful; man could progress upwards if he avoided temptation and allowed nature to purge the worst and save the best. Was there not still "space as spaciousness" offering total possibility to the American Adam? From questioning, Norris was now to move to affirmation. In his most important novel, *The Octopus*, he was to give his blessing to progress through the workings of an evolutionary nature.

In a sense, the novel is an autobiographical expression of the author's philosophical quest during the 1890's. It begins with Presley, a poet who has come to California to write the great American poem. He believes that he can find the inspiration for this epic only in the West because there "A new race, a new people—hardy, brave, and passionate—were building an empire; where the tumultuous life ran like fire from dawn to dark, and from dark to dawn again, primitive, brutal, honest and without fear."

Presley represents the faith of Jacksonian America. He has fled the cities and factories which have brought complexity even into the Midwest; hoping to find in the last frontier of the Pacific coast a final outpost, an oasis of virgin land, where this faith can be restored. He wants the inspiration of Jefferson's republic with its promise of timeless harmony, wants to recapture its faith in a nature which is serene in its completeness, to find inspiration for his poem in a dream that Norris claims never was and never can be. Presley is presented as a romantic who is persuaded that his fantasy expressed the reality of nature.

Norris was now attempting a counterinitiation of the nation into another reality through the experience of the poet. Presley has taken up residence on a wheat ranch in a vast fertile valley of California in order to achieve organic harmony with nature. But he cannot write. His farmer friends are not living in harmony with the good earth; even here on the last frontier, eastern complexity has disturbed the spontaneous equilibrium of man and land. Into this last vestige of the American Garden, there has crept a serpent, an octopus, the railroad. The disharmony of artificial, man-made culture, is corrupting the West. For Presley, there can be no American poem in the midst of disharmony; the promise of America has been that of progress away from the corrupt complexity of Europe. And now America has proved to be without uniqueness; the New World was no different from the Old. There could be no poem about a "new race," a "new people," no song of a "tumultuous life. . . . primitive, brutal, honest, and without fear."

All was lost for Presley unless this small band of farmers, the last American free men, began a second American revolution which would destroy the octopus and lift the tyranny of human institutions from the land. The railroad was "the symbol of a vast power, huge, terrible, flinging the echo of its thunder over all the reaches of the valley." Smashing through a flock of sheep, smashing through American innocence, "leaving blood and destruction in its path," this was "the leviathan, with tentacles of steel clutching into the soil, the soulless Force, the iron-hearted Power, the Monster, the Colossus, the Octopus."

Presley had achieved a vision of doom through technological progress which paralleled that of Mark Twain. But he still remained true to his Jacksonian principles, to a belief in progress away from complexity to simplicity. Human institutions were artificial; they had no intrinsic strength. Farmers, men of the soil, were so strengthened by nature that even this small band of embattled men might begin to turn the tide and destroy the vast urban-industrial frontier which had spread from Europe across the East and ever farther west.

For Presley, the railroad represented a financial conspiracy by evil men. The farmers had only to fight a parasitical alien like the railroad representative, S. Behrman, "a large, fat man, with a great stomach; his cheek and the upper part of his thick neck ran together to form a great tremulous jowl, shaven and blue-grey in colour; a roll of fat, sprinkled with sparse hair, moist in perspiration, protruded over the back of his collar."

On the other hand the rancher, Magnus Derrick, seemed to Presley like one of the patriot leaders who inspired their neighbors in that spring of 1775 to take a stand against British tyranny. "Here in this corner of a great nation, here, on the edge of the continent, here in this valley of the West, far from the great centres, isolated, remote, lost, the great iron hand crushes life from us, crushes liberty. . . . Yet it is Lexington—God help us, God enlighten us. God rouse us from our lethargy—it is Lexington; farmers with guns in their hands fighting for liberty. . . . is it not symbolical of the great and terrible conflict that is going on everywhere in these United States?"

How fortunate, as Presley reported the impending battle between the farmers with guns and the paid bullies of Behrman, that these brave and simple men were led by Magnus Derrick who had his roots in the Jeffersonian republic. Here "was the last protest of the Old School, rising up there in denunciation of the new order of things, the statesman opposed to the politician; honesty, rectitude. Uncompromising integrity prevailing for the last time against the devious maneuvering, the evil communications, the rotten expediency of a corrupted institution."

Before the poet's horrified eyes, the farmers are shot down behind their barricades, their lands are taken, their widows and orphans driven into poverty, even prostitution. The evil Behrman has triumphed, and Presley witnesses the total destruction of his dream. But hope springs eternal and now he comes to believe that Magnus Derrick and his fellow-farmers were not crushed by the Octopus, the juggernaut of nineteenth-century technology. It was nature, the West itself which has defeated them.

He remembers the cry of Magnus Derrick: "For one moment to be able to strike back, to crush his enemy, to defeat the railroad, hold the corporation in the grip of his fist, put down S. Behrman, rehabilitate himself, regain his self-respect. To be once more powerful, to command, to dominate."

Surely here was no love of nature, no real desire for harmony. How was Derrick truly different from Behrman? Was it not true that "For all his public spirit, for all his championship of justice and truth, his respect for law, Magnus remained the gambler, willing to play for colossal stakes. . . . It was in this frame of mind that Magnus and the multitude of other ranchers, of whom he was a type, farmed their ranches. They had no love for their land. They were not attached to the soil. . . . to get all there was out of the land, to squeeze it dry, to exhaust it, seemed their policy. When, at last, the land was worn out, would refuse to yield, they would invest their money in something else."

Presley was no longer able to read American history as a dramatic conflict between virtuous people and corrupt interests. He could see now only one reality beneath all the masquerade of human pretensions. Nature remained. Nature was the only reality! But what was the identity of this nature which had crushed those who tried to exploit her?

Norris wanted to reassure his readers that if nature was not static and harmonious, it was nonetheless benevolent and redemptive. He wanted them to have faith that a living, dynamic nature was making evolutionary progress toward an ultimate good and that this process, while it might appear superficially dreadful and cruel, was necessary to man's salvation.

This is the authentic nature that Presley discovers when he abandons his eighteenth-century concept that was sterile in its deathlike and rigid permanence. He has begun to find a new theme for his poem about the West, a West which symbolized a vibrant, vital growing nature. "Deep down there in the recesses of the soil, the great heart throbbed once more. Thrilling with passion, vibrating with desire, offering itself to the career of the plough, insistent, eager, imperious. Dimly one felt the deep-seated tremble of the earth, the uneasy agitation of its members, the hidden tumult of its womb, demanding to be made fruitful, to reproduce, to disengage the eternal renascent germ of Life that stirred and struggled in its loins."

The West was not people, fallible and corrupt; it was nature, strong and fertile. It was only in the seasons of the earth itself that there was significant drama. All human actions, all history was meaningless. Presley is prepared to believe Shelgrim, president of the railroad, when he tells him that there is no octopus, that no human was responsible for the suffering of the farmers; the railroad is only a necessary adjunct of nature, necessary to distribute the fruits of her loins: "It rang with clear reverberation of truth. Was no one to blame for the horror? Forces . . . were these then the enemies, after all? Not enemies, there was no malevolence in nature.

"Men . . . were shot down in the very noon of life, hearts were broken, little children started in life lamentably handicapped; young girls were brought to a life of shame; old women died in the heart of life for lack of food. In that little isolated group of human insects, misery, death, and anguish spun like a wheel of fire. But the wheat remained. Untouched, unassailable, undefiled, that mighty world force . . . wrapped in nirvanic calm . . . moved onward in its appointed grooves. . . .

"Falseness dies; injustice and oppression . . . fade and vanish away; greed, cruelty, selfishness, and inhumanity, are short-lived; the individual suffers but the race goes on. . . . The larger view always and through all shams, all wickednesses, discovers the truth that will, in the end, prevail, and all things, surely, inevitably, work together for good."

Presley was ready, at last, to write his poem of the West. He would tell Americans to surrender their pride of independence and perfection and throw themselves on the mercy of nature, to be humble and wait for nature to make them better. The ranchers, under the leadership of Magnus Derrick, had struggled to control the wheat for their own profit, and they were defeated. Behrman had conspired to use the railroad for personal profit, and the wheat killed him. To achieve salvation, men must turn away from culture, from civilization where they are corrupted by their pride in their artificial creations, must come naked and unashamed to nature and follow wherever it leads. Only then might the promise of total possibility for an American Adam be fulfilled.

## 2

The tragedy which Stephen Crane saw implicit in the American destiny was of a very different order from that predicted by Mark Twain. For Twain, the tragedy lay in the loss of natural innocences as the nation slipped back into the artificial culture of civilization. His conviction of social disaster took form slowly during the 1870's and became crystallized only by 1890. These were the first twenty years of Stephen Crane's life, when Americans still felt as free to live by the laws of nature as they had felt in 1830. The American slum could not be compared to Tom Canty's medieval London, because the latter was caused by the tyranny of man whereas the former was due to the laws of nature which must eliminate the weak and the evil and uplift the strong and the good. Man was being saved from his inner weakness by the liberating forces of evolution.

During the 1890's, the remaining ten years of his life and his only years of maturity and artistic creativity, Stephen Crane repected the complacent doctrine of Social Darwinism. But his intellectual world, his imaginative projection of reality, remained within the boundaries of the Jacksonian and Darwinian views of nature. Rejecting both, he was left with the individual who exists in space where nothing is possible. Like Norris, he was prepared to show that the perfect innocence of the American Garden did not exist, but unlike him, he saw no progressive upward movement through survival of the fittest. Indeed, life held no meaning, yet Crane asked that men not surrender to despair but do battle against the impersonal forces of the universe and treat their comrades in the struggle with love and compassion. The individual must face the indifference of the universe with stoic strength, knowing that there was no reward but personal dignity. Man must cherish the memory of a loving God even with the awful knowledge that he would lose every battle and ultimately be engulfed by the forces of darkness.

When Crane wrote his first novel, *Maggie*, at the age of twenty, he had not yet achieved the strength of this code of courage. He came to this book burning with a sense of loss and outraged at the weakness in human nature which made a heavenly city impossible. In another context, he has provided a perfect analysis of his own motivation in writing *Maggie*: "When it occurs to a man that nature does not regard him as important, and that she feels she would not maim the universe by disposing of him, he at first wishes to throw bricks at the temple, and he hates deeply the fact that there are no bricks and no temples."

Maggie is the child of the city slum, who had "blossomed in a mud puddle. She grew to be a most rare and wonderful production of a tenement district, a pretty girl. None of the dirt of Rum Alley seemed to be in her veins." In Crane's slum of 1890, the emphasis is not on the indifference of the universe but on the vitality of human evil. Maggie, the symbol of the American dream of innocence, is brought into dramatic contrast with the reality of human hellishness. And the devil is represented by her mother. Thus Crane strikes directly at the heart of nineteeth-century gentility. For American Victorians, men might compromise but women as mothers were eternal and immutabe virgins leading their children upward along a path of brightest virtue.

We meet Maggie's mother after her nightly drunken brawl with her husband; the American Garden has become the American inferno. "A glow from the fire threw red lines over the bare floor, the cracked and soiled plastering, and the overturned and broken furniture. In the middle of the floor lay his mother asleep. In one corner of the room his father's limp body hung across the seat of a chair. . . . Her face was inflamed and swollen from drinking. Her yellow brows shaded eyelids that had grown blue. Her tangled hair tossed in waves over her forehead. Her mouth was set in the same lines of vindictive hatred that it had, perhaps, borne during the fight. Her bare red arms were thrown out above her head . . . like that of a sated villain. . . . The small frame of the ragged girl was quivering. Her features were haggard from weeping, and her eyes gleamed with fear . . . [as she and her brother huddled in a corner] the eyes of both were drawn, by the same force to stare at the woman's face, for they thought she need only to awake and all the fiends would come from below."

As the child grows toward womanhood in this atmosphere of brutality, she dreams of escape. In her fantasy, a Prince Charming would rescue her from her dungeon. The prince would carry her away from the city into the countryside where she would be given a vine-covered cottage for sanctuary, and the beautiful flowers and the exquisite song of the birds would so fill her mind that she would never remember her childhood. This was the American dream of innocence and redemptive nature. But, for Crane, Maggie could never be rescued; the dream was false. She goes to work in a sweatshop, and her imagination transforms Pete, the bartender, into a romantic hero. She puts her fate into his hands and is compromised and abandoned.

The people of the tenements turn their backs on Maggie, not because she has lost her virtue but because she has failed to transcend the reality of their existence. No one will reach out a hand to help her. She has only one path to follow in the vast, cold, impersonal city. Quietly she walks through the darkness of the night and steps unnoticed into the still deeper darkness of the river. There is no place for innocence in the world of reality.

How should his readers react to this metaphorical destruction of the American Garden? Did Crane intend that they turn to cynicism and despair like Maggie's brother and mother? Clearly and emphatically, Crane answers no in the sequel, *George's Mother*. The allegory of innocence lost must lead men to face reality with courage. Above all, Americans must not feel sorry for themselves, must not feel cheated in being expelled from the Jeffersonian covenant. If coldness and impersonality are the fundamental characteristics of the universe, they must not try to escape into fantasy and romance.

We meet George Kelsey on the streets of New York, "a brown young man . . . puffing at a corn-cob pipe. His shoulders had a self-reliant poise." Here is the American Adam who has lost his idyllic home in the American countryside. Every root with his rural past has been cut, and George and his mother have been forced to come to the city, where they will try to preserve the myth of innocence. Unlike Maggie's mother, George's represents all the mothers of the nineteenth-century fantasy of human perfection. She is determined to keep her son the good country boy in spite of the hostility of the urban environment with its manifold temptations for evil.

The dream of arcadian simplicity has dissolved into the reality of the urban nightmare. This is the setting for the moral testing of the last American Adam, George Kelsey. It is easy to stand with squared shoulders in honest self-reliance and independence in the world of the Jeffersonian dream. But can George remain a man in a world which is not designed especially for his ease and comfort? Can he have strength and courage even as he becomes aware that he is not one of God's chosen? He becomes one of a group which meets regularly to drink away their sorrows. Here: "Each man explained, in his way, that he was totally out of place in the before-mentioned world. They were possessed of various virtues which were unappreciated by those with whom they were commonly obliged to mingle; they were fitted for a tree-shaded land where everything was peace."

Castrated by self-pity, George becomes a victim of the city, incapable of any meaningful action. In his tenement, there is a pretty girl, Maggie. He dreams of winning her hand and of carrying her back into the rural past. He will not approach her, however, until he has the power to transcend the poverty and ugliness of the city and to restore the agrarian garden. "Occasionally he wondered how fate was going to begin making an enormous figure of him; but he had no doubt of the result. A chariot of pink clouds was coming for him. His faith was his reason for existence. Meanwhile he could dream of the indefinite woman and the fragrance of roses that came from her hair." One day, a sharply dressed young man from the city takes Maggie away from her drunken mother. "During the next few days Kelsey suffered from his first gloomy conviction that the earth was not grateful to him for his presence upon it." Maggie never returned; there would be no Eve for the American Adam in the urban jungle.

George's mother still stubbornly clings to her faith that God would deliver her and her son from the evils of the city, but the faith of this symbolic nineteenth-century mother was useless to her son. Her faith in the reality of her past could comfort her last days; she was old, and she could live with memories. But her son was young and must live in the city. He must find the foundation for a constructive, creative life within this environment.

Crane captures all of the irrelevance and impotence of the mother's faith when she forces George to come with her to church. What appears to her the very citadel of strength is immediately apprehended by her son as a symbol of weakness and death. "In a dark street the little chapel sat humbly between two towering apartment houses. A red street-lamp stood in front. It threw a marvellous reflection upon the wet pavements. It was like the death-stain of a spirit. Farther up, the brilliant lights of an avenue made a span of gold across the black street. A roar of wheels and a clangor of bells came from this point, interwoven into a sound emblematic of the life of the city. It seemed somehow to affront the solemn and austere little edifice. It suggested an approaching barbaric invasion. The little church, pierced, would die with a fine illimitable scorn for its slayers."

In *Maggie* and *George's Mother*, Crane used the city to symbolize the reality of a universe that had no relationship to the nineteenth-century belief in a beneficent, redemptive harmonious nature. He was not agreeing with Twain that Americans had exchanged heaven for hell by exchanging nature for technology. Rather he used the new urban environment to symbolize what he believed was the impersonal cruelty of nature. This was the real environment of man now. Jeffersonian America had been a dream, a romantic fantasy, through which men had tried to escape from reality. Now that the urban-industrial frontier was destroying the plausibility of the fantasy, Americans felt they had lost "something tangible and substantial." But, for Crane, all they had lost was a dream born of cowardice which encouraged still greater cowardice. His only escape from despair was to face unflinchingly the reality of a meaningless universe. As he wrote in one of his letters, "From this moment to that deathbed may be a short time or a long one but at any rate it means a life of labor and sorrow. I do not confront it blithely. I confront it with desperate resolution. There is not even much hope in my attitude. I do not even expect to do good. But I expect to make a sincere, desperate, lonely battle to remain true to my conception of my life and the way it should be lived."

In this battle the individual was doomed to ultimate defeat, but he could triumph over his own cowardice. "For the first time I saw the majestic forces which are arrayed against man's true success . . . man's own colossal impulses were stronger than chains, and I perceived that the fight was not going to be with the world but with myself."* The dignity of the individual comes from the sublimation of cowardice. Americans, however, came to this struggle with a still greater handicap, that of a cultural dream which told them that the natural state of man was peace: this was Crane's lesson for himself and his countrymen—war was man's normal environment.

It is with this purpose that he wrote his masterpiece, *The Red Badge of Courage.* The allegorical setting of this novel is as brilliantly chosen as were those of *Maggie* and *George's Mother.* For Twain and Howells, as for most Americans, the Civil War marked the end of the Jeffersonian republic of simplicity and virtue and the beginning of the new frontier of complexity and evil. *The Red Badge of Courage* is the story of the initiation of one young man, Henry Fleming, into the awful truth that even in America the eternal environment for man is war. But the experience transcends a particular war and a specific hero; it represents the experience of an entire nation.

Henry Fleming's youthful imagination is almost totally divorced from reality. In his romantic view he is a free spirit who was enlisted for service to help destroy an enemy which had disturbed the peace of the nation. He is a knight in shining armor who will courageously destroy the dragon that had invaded the peaceable kingdom, and then ride home to live happily ever after, sure that the nation will be able to slumber in eternal security.

When Henry joins the army, however, he has joined the human race, the reality of human existence. He has stepped out of the realm of fantasy. The army exists; it

---

*Stephen Crane, *Love Letter to Nellie Crouse* (Syracuse University Press, 1954).

does not move swiftly and dramatically to destroy dragons; Henry begins to have the feeling that he has joined an organization which will continue to exist forever—that there is nothing it can do to end the war. This is Crane's human society engaged in eternal warfare, and it is against this brute reality that Henry rebels. As the American Adam he feels that he has the right to total freedom, total possibility. But "he instantly saw that it would be impossible for him to escape from the regiment. It enclosed him. . . . He was in a moving box." He reacts with fear and frustration as this impersonal organization begins to force him toward the battlefield. Why was he here? He hadn't made the war, and "he had not enlisted of his free will. He had been dragged by the merciless government. And now they were taking him out to be slaughtered." What could he do to escape this social machine, officered by insensitive robots, which took him step by step toward the battle in which he recognized he had no personal commitment? "It was useless to expect appreciation of his profound and fine senses from such men as the lieutenant."

Once the battle begins, Henry suddenly finds courage in the bravery of his comrades. He had reached the battlefield alienated from the men in his ranks. But now as these nameless soldiers face death without flinching, he begins to feel identity with the mass: "He suddenly lost concern for himself, and forgot to look at a menacing fate. He became not a man but a member. He felt that something of which he was a part—a regiment, an army, a cause, or a country— was in crisis. He was welded into a common personality. . . . He felt the subtle battle brotherhood more potent even than the cause for which they were fighting. It was a mysterious fraternity born of the smoke and danger of death."

Then the line breaks, the solidarity disintegrates; the men run, and Henry runs with them. Like the others, he could be brave, and like them he could be a coward. But he cannot admit that he shares the common weakness of all men; he had run only because the others had. Isolated in the forest during the retreat, he further rationalizes his cowardice. After all, some had remained on the firing line when the panic began. Henry is sure he would have been one of those if only his immediate neighbors had not run and given him the impression that the whole regiment was in retreat.

But even as he tries to justify his flight to solitude, he recognizes that he cannot remain a deserter from the army, separated from the rest of mankind, and he comes out of hiding to join the ranks of the wounded. In the midst of these men who had faced the enemy more bravely than he had, his self-pity turns to shame. "He wished that he, too, had a wound, a red badge of courage." As he marches in their company, he falls in step with the tall soldier beside whom he had marched into battle—a man who had symbolized courage for him. Now he learns that this friend had fought bravely but with fear in his heart just as he himself had. And so he becomes aware that he was not separated from these men by his cowardice. All men are cowards, but the brave control their fear and accept the battle as inevitable.

Henry's initiation is completed. He has given up the fantasy of his childhood that there was a refuge of perpetual peace and harmony to which one could withdraw after successfully defeating the enemy. There was no such refuge. No one could desert from this struggle. The only choice the individual had was to face the unseen enemy with dignity, or flinch and find excuse for his cowardice in self-pity. Spiritually, Henry had become one of those wounded; he had lost the innocence of childhood and had gained the resolution of manhood. When he receives an accidental blow that gives him, too, a visible red badge of courage which links him with the other veterans, "He felt a quiet manhood, non-assertive but of a sturdy and strong blood. He knew that he would no more quail before his guides wherever they should point. . . . He was a man."

# 3

Theodore Dreiser, like his contemporaries, Stephen Crane and Frank Norris, was obesssed by the problem of innocence within the context of the new national faith in an evolutionary universe. If he could not follow Crane in the rejection of this revised promise of progress, neither could he go along with the acceptance of Frank Norris, who saw the lot of the individual of small moment in the upward thrust of nature. For Dreiser, the suffering of the individual was important; uncertainty and tragedy must remain part of the human situation until evolution in some far distant time should have brought man and his environment into harmony. His faith in progress seems never to have reached rocklike certainty. He, too, was haunted by thoughts of the meaninglessness of human existence and the indifference of the universe toward the tragedies of individual lives, but he accepted the possibility of the survival of innocence in a world that does move, even if in an exceedingly slow and confused fashion, toward an ultimate spiritual fulfillment.

*Sister Carrie*, his first novel, expresses all of these tensions. Here once again an American author confronts the question of whether innocence can be preserved when the Eden of the Jeffersonian republic is destroyed and the fallibility of human nature is realized. Carrie is eighteen, the symbol of nineteenth-century virtue, when she is forced out of the protective environment of the small town and comes to the urban jungle of Chicago. Like Crane's Maggie, she dreams of liberation from her sweatshop job, is betrayed by the man she loves. But from the moment she becomes aware of her betrayal, her story diverges from that of Maggie. Her path leads to increasing personal success and fulfillment, not toward death.

*Sister Carrie* is basically a metaphysical novel, and it

is surprising that literary critics have ignored its explicit
meaning. Here is Dreiser's own philosophical statement:

"To those who have never wavered in conscience, the
predicament of the individual whose mind is less strongly
constituted and who trembles in the balance between duty
and desire is scarcely appreciable. . . . Not alone in sensitive,
highly organized natures is such a mental conflict possible.
The dullest specimen of humanity, when drawn by desire
toward evil, is recalled by a sense of right, which is pro-
portionate in power and strength to his evil tendency. We
must remember that it may not be a knowledge of right, for
no knowledge of right is predicated on the animal's instinctive recoil at evil. Men are still led by instinct before they
are regulated by knowledge. . . . Our civilization is still in
a middle stage, scarcely beast, in that it is no longer wholly
guided by instinct; scarcely human, in that it is not yet
wholly guided by reason. . . . We see man far removed from
the lairs of the jungles, his innate instincts dulled by too
near an approach to free will, his free will not sufficiently
developed to replace his instincts and afford him perfect
guidance. He is becoming too wise to harken always to
instincts and desires; he is still too weak to always prevail
against them. As a beast, the forces of life aligned him with
them, as a man, he has not wholly learned to align himself
with the forces. In this intermediate stage he wavers—
neither drawn in harmony with nature by his instincts nor
yet wisely putting himself into harmony with his own free
will. . . . We have the consolation of knowing that evolution
is ever in action, that the ideal is a light that cannot fail."

For Dreiser's Carrie there is meaning in the universe,
and innocence is protected. "The unintellectual are not so
helpless. Nature has taught the beasts of the field to fly when
some unheralded danger threatens. . . . 'He keepeth His
creatures whole,' was not written of the beasts alone. Carrie
was unwise, and therefore, like the sheep in its unwisdom,
strong in feeling." She was able to find enough beauty in

existence to keep her will to live. The things of this world were enough for her, even though, at the end of the story, she is bewildered and lonely, unfulfilled because she does not understand. "Sitting alone, she was now an illustration of the devious ways by which one who feels rather than reasons, may be led in this pursuit of beauty. . . . Know, then, that for you is neither surfeit or content. In your rocking chair, by your window, shall you dream such happiness as you may never feel."

The truly tragic figure in the novel is Hurstwood because he has the power to choose, and it is this freedom of choice which leads him to suicide. Like all men of his generation, Dreiser is concerned with the power of the sexual drive. For him, as for Norris, it is unchecked sexual appetite in the male which makes him a brute. Charles Drouet, Carrie's early seducer, "could not help what he was going to do. He could not see clearly enough to wish to do differently. He was drawn by his innate desire to act his old pursuing part. He would need to delight himself with Carrie as surely as he would need to eat his heavy breakfast."

Hurstwood, however, is different. He is not the prisoner of his lower instincts. He has achieved the power of choice. But he is symbolic of the tragedy of modern civilization which has not yet learned to will itself into harmony with nature. Hurstwood is the civilized man who has used his limited power of choice to build an artificial culture; most of his sensitivity is directed toward his self-made upward climb in society. "If Hurstwood had one leaning, it was toward notabilities. He considered that, if anywhere, he belonged among them. He was too proud to toady, too keen not to strictly observe the plane he occupied when there were those present who did not appreciate him, but, in situations like the present, where he could shine as a gentleman and be received without equivocation as a friend and equal among men of known ability, he was most delighted."

Yet Hurstwood is sensitive enough to be discontented

with mere social success. Instinctively, he wants more, though "he wavers—neither drawn to harmony with nature by his instincts nor yet wisely putting himself into harmony by his own free will." He wants to marry Carrie but to divorce his wife would mean the end of his job, the collapse of his hard-won economic and social position. A prey to indecision, one day he finds the office safe unlocked. While he counts the money and considers the possibility of flight with Carrie, the safe accidentally locks leaving him with the money in his hands. Chance has made the choice for him.

Hurstwood goes from strength to weakness, from independence to dependence on Carrie. He becomes impotent in every way while she becomes more self-confident and successful. When Carrie finally leaves him, his emptiness is complete. His suicide is the last act in the tragedy of a man of Dreiser's middle stage of civilization, unable to live by the heart or the head, exiled from the social structure which had provided him with his only security.

Two quotations from Dreiser's next novel, *Jennie Gerhardt,* dramatize his continuing commitment to the theme of natural innocence and civilized confusion. Jennie is a girl who will be protected from harm because "Nature is not ungenerous. Its winds and stars are fellows with you. Let the soul be gentle and receptive, and this vast truth will come home—not in set phrases, perhaps, but as a feeling, a comfort, which after all, is the last essence of knowledge. In the universe, peace is wisdom." Her lover, Lester Kane, is a civilized man who is threatened by society for keeping Jennie outside the bonds of matrimony. "So well defined is the sphere of social activity that he who departs from it is doomed."

In these two novels which celebrated the triumph of feminine instinct over the threatening social forces, Dreiser established a philosophical position markedly different from that of Crane and Norris. In a significant sense, he was closer to the realists, Twain, Howells, and James, than were his two contemporaries. The controlling metaphor in Crane's writing was the coldness of nature. Society was largely irrelevant to the concerns of his individuals; the drama in their lives was the way they confronted the dark universe, either with cowardice or courage. For Norris, society was important only in the sense that it tempted the individual to selfish ends and obscured the importance of nature. His courageous individual should transcend society to accept the laws of necessity; disharmony was necessary and good because it represented the progressive process of evolution.

Dreiser, however, found disharmony to be the product of society rather than of nature. Like the realists, he saw the fallibility of the individual as the source of social confusion. He could not write, as Norris had in *The Octopus*, that it was possible for the individual to reject society once he had seen the beckoning light of nature. But also he could not accept the conclusion of the realists that society was the only environmental influence on man. In a primitive past, man had lived in Eden, governed by instincts which had kept him in harmony with nature. But this was an Eden without dignity for man because he did not choose the good. Then the process of evolution had taken man out of the realm of instinct and given him the power of choice. This faculty was not yet perfected, and imperfect man, unable to have instinctive harmony, built society to give himself stability and security. The ultimate goal was to achieve the perfect stability and security of harmony with nature, by a perfected faculty of free will. Then once more, man should be in Eden but with the dignity of free choice and conscience.

Dreiser saw modern man in constant conflict because of his dual commitment to society and nature. He was not yet ready to live without society but his conscience told him that he must not remain within the limited and relative values of the community. He must strive for union with nature. In

*Sister Carrie*, he had suggested that a woman may be a primitive link with the instinctive Eden of the past. Carrie, however, had a masculine ambition, almost aggressiveness, which kept her from that complete "peace" which Dreiser considered to be ultimate wisdom. But Jennie Gerhardt had "a soul" which was "gentle and receptive," and she found harmony with the universe. "Did anything matter except goodness—goodness of heart? What else was there that was real?"

From the maudlin world of Jennie Gerhardt, Dreiser shifted his emphasis to the virile world of Frank Cowperwood in *The Titan* and *The Financier*. The shift was from the triumph of the eternal woman to the tragedy of the temporal man, even a superman.

For Dreiser there are two kinds of men: the average "petty piece of machinery," who believes that the artificial social structure is infallible in its stability, and the man of superior intellect. "Life to him, as to every other man of large practical knowledge and insight, was an inexplicable tangle. What were you going to do about the so-called morals and precepts of the world? . . . There were people who believed in some esoteric standard of right—some ideal of conduct absolutely and very far removed from practical life; but he had never seen them practice it save to their own financial (not moral—he would not say that) destruction. They were never significant, practical men who clung to those fatuous ideals. They were always poor, nondescript, negligible dreamers."

For Frank Cowperwood there was no valid law or ethics in the institutions of society; only the strong survived.

What is the moral of the rise and fall of this ruthless, dynamic individual? Accepting the hypocrisy of the social order, Cowperwood uses it in a Machiavellian fashion to achieve personal success. "One found oneself in a given social order, theory, or scheme of things. For purposes of social success, in order not to offend, to smooth one's path, make things easy, avoid useless criticism and the like, it was necessary to create an outward seeming—ostensibly conform. Beyond that it was necessary to do nothing. Never fail, never get caught." Cowperwood reminded Dreiser of the black grouper, the fish that was able to adapt its coloration to any environment and easily catch the fish of simple and permanent hue.

But if Cowperwood devoured the little men who were gulled by their belief in society's laws and morals, this did not mean that society did not have power. Cowperwood could manipulate within society, but he could not escape from it, and this is why after every success he was defeated. Precisely because he was superior, because he did not take the values of society seriously, he could find no real fulfillment in exploiting the artificial laws of the community for his personal advantage. "He was not without sensibilities of the highest order, only they were governed and controlled in him by that cold iron thing, his reason, which never forsook him."

Cowperwood, the businessman, used his reason to advance his financial interests. But the irony was that, to the extent that he was the rational businessman rather than the individual of highest sensibilities, he was fulfilling the moral values of his society which held that to make money was the greatest achievement. He was never more the prisoner of society than when he believed he was a lawless, dynamic, self-sufficient, and self-reliant individual.

At the same time he lived by the heart as well as the head. "Of all individuals, he respected, indeed revered, the sincere artist. Existence was a mystery, but these souls who set themselves to quiet tasks of beauty had caught something of which he was divinely conscious. Life had touched them with a wisdom, their hearts and souls were attuned to sweet harmonies of which the common world knew nothing." Cowperwood sensed the existence of natural harmony beneath the disharmony of society; the reality of nature beneath the artificiality of culture.

Actually, passion not reason was the cause of Cowperwood's collisions in the business world. He had no use for the "grasping legality of established matrimony"; for him "the ultimate end of fame, power, vigor was beauty, and that beauty was a compound of the taste, the emotion, the innate culture, passion, and dreams of a woman like Bernice Fleming." But there is no permanent escape possible from the artificial disharmony of society to the harmony of nature. Cowperwood can pursue beauty but he cannot possess it, and just as he loses one mistress after another, so he must also be punished by society for his efforts to transcend it. "Rushing like a great comet to the zenith, his path a blazing trail, Cowperwood did for the hour illuminate the terrors and wonders of individuality. But for him also the eternal equation—the pathos of the discovery that even giants are but pygmies, and that an ultimate balance must be struck."

This tension which a superior man must experience, caught between the demands of society that he conform to its temporal standards and the urge of his instincts to transcend its ephemeral values, is given lengthy philosophical expression in Dreiser's autobiographical novel, *The Genius*. Eugene Witla is no more able to escape the demands of his society than was Frank Cowperwood; his "conscience unmotivated by cold self-interest" binds him to those moral conventions which Cowperwood derided. He is trapped in marriage, doubly trapped by sex and the mores of society, gives up his art and falls for the lure of success; he becomes a responsible citizen. But "he was always thinking . . . that life was somehow bigger and subtler and darker than any given theory or order of living. It might well be worthwhile for a man or a woman to be honest or moral within a given condition or quality of society, but it did not matter at all in the ultimate substance and composition of the universe . . .

they meant nothing in the shifting, subtle forces of nature. They were just accidental harmonies."

Like Cowperwood, Witla achieves success, and like the financier feels that his life is empty, without meaning. Once again a Dreiser hero is undone by scandal; catastrophe follows in the wake of passion that gives meaning to his existence yet contravenes the established order of society.

From the loss of his wife and mistress, Eugene Witla emerges with a new ability to realize himself as an artist; for the first time he is able to see his life in its proper perspective. The disharmonies of convention, symbolized by his wife, and his love for his young mistress were both parts of a meaningful metaphysical pattern. Witla had intuitively sensed the imperfections of this world. But he still had to play his part as a man among men "pulling this wagon of evolution."

He wanted to believe that "When mortal man blends his thoughts of existence with the spiritual, and works only as God works, he will no longer grope in the dark and cling to earth because he has not tasted heaven." But instead he accepted the views of "Darwin, Huxley . . . a whole string of British thinkers who . . . showed him a beauty, a formality, a lavishness of form and idea in nature's methods which fairly transfigured him. . . . Truly there were hierarchies and powers as Alfred Russell Wallace pointed out. There was a God somewhere. He was on His throne."

At the end of the novel, Eugene Witla is at peace in the world, no longer tempted by either convention or sex. He has brought himself into harmony with the universe, and thus achieved the highest dignity which could come to man. Through his will and intelligence he has reached that union with nature which Sister Carrie and Jennie Gerhardt had approached instinctively. By World War I, Dreiser had found the philosophic formula which gave him sufficient faith in evolutionary nature to endure the disharmony of society.

# IV

---

# THE LOST GENERATION

---

*Winston Churchill*
*Ernest Hemingway*
*F. Scott Fitzgerald*

Between 1900 and 1917, Americans were inclined to reject the outlook of both the realists and the naturalists. Presumably they had found an answer to the complexity of the late nineteenth century, which promised to restore the Jeffersonian covenant with an eternally harmonious nature; the peaceable kingdom seemed within reach.

This was the progressive era, when Americans discovered that progress had not been fulfilled in 1828. Historical complexity had remained the dominant environment throughout the nineteenth century; but now, in the first years of the twentieth, civilization would re-create the natural order, and the promise of the New World Garden would finally be fulfilled.

This new millennial faith, which made the viewpoints of Norris, Crane, and Dreiser as well as Twain, Howells, and James seem irrelevant, was expressed with both precision and poetic power by the historian, Charles Beard. As a young man he had left the Indiana prairie in the 1890's to travel in Europe because it was there that one could study the roots of the forces of industrialism and urbanism which were so rapidly conquering the frontier of virgin land. He was not persuaded that Americans must see the chaos of modern society as either a return to European history or the expression of natural evolution. In Germany and especially in England, he found evidence for the hopeful report which he was to bring home.

Industrialism, Beard proposed, should not be thought of as an expression of civilization making for complexity, but rather as a frontier force. Inevitably it would destroy complexity and make for simplicity. The coming of industrialism, therefore, did not mean the end of the American dream; on the contrary, it guaranteed the salvation of our national faith.

Once, during the seventeenth and eighteenth centuries, something like an American Garden had existed. Man, as the eighteenth-century *philosophes* had maintained, is instinctively good; he is corrupted only by traditions and institutions. When Europeans stepped out of feudalism to live in the New World state of nature, they were redeemed. Reborn, they had become the American Adam. But the great error of George Bancroft and his contemporaries, according to Beard, was that the older historians had seen mankind oppressed almost entirely by the social structure of medieval civilization. Bancroft seemingly was not aware that by 1776 Europe was dominated by a new and equally corrupt civilization, that of capitalism. He had not realized that there was an American aristocracy in the 1770's and 1780's, which represented English capitalist culture, and which would work to frustrate an agrarian people's desire to throw off every vestige of Old World civilization.

It was true that Bancroft had seen a conflict between the American people and this alien, parasitical aristocracy. But, Beard argued, he did not understand that this group had destroyed the democratic autonomy of the people by creating institutional hierarchy in the Constitution. Not only

Jefferson but even Jackson had not been able to destroy the institutional power of the eastern elite; by the 1830's, these foreign-influenced capitalists had used their control of the national government to make their form of economy dominant. The freedom and the innocence of the Jeffersonian yeoman were not regained under Jackson. Instead they were lost permanently to the finance capitalists of Boston, New York, and Philadelphia.

For Beard, Mark Twain was wrong in seeing business and industry as a single entity. Business was artificial. As an alien complex of institutions and traditions, it introduced disharmony into the peaceful agrarian communities of the colonial past. But industrialism was natural; it was a productive force comparable to the land itself. Looking at the disharmony introduced by business, Norris had argued that it expressed the disharmonious structure of nature. But, Beard affirmed, nature is not disharmonious. Man is capable of living in peaceful harmony with any natural productive force.

And this was the great virtue of industrialism. It was a natural productive force with which man could achieve organic and peaceful union. But it was also a naturally destructive force which inevitably destroyed all man-made institutions and traditions. This meant, Beard prophesied, the inexorable destruction of all the complexity of European capitalist culture which the founding fathers, that conspiratorial eastern aristocracy, had used to ravage the Garden of the colonial past and to send the American Adam back into the horror of historical turmoil. The American experience in the immediate future was to be that of a new liberating frontier—that of industrialism, which would re-create timeless harmony.

By 1912, Beard saw the political triumph of the people led by the representative hero, Theodore Roosevelt. Throughout the nineteenth century, the people had been kept from power by the political parties and the professional politicians who were agents of Wall Street. Now, however, as the people began to gain strength from industrialism, as they were fused into a single massive unity, they were expressing their will spontaneously in the nonpartisan Progressive party. For Beard, as for Bancroft, the people were not sacrificing their innocence in coming to political power; they were pledged to use this power only to purge and purify, to regain simplicity—not to create complexity.

Even though he was disappointed by the victory of Woodrow Wilson in 1912, he retained his faith in the inevitable victory of the people; the frontier force of industrialism could not be halted. He would use his historical scholarship to hasten the inexorable defeat of the eastern aristocracy. The major defense of this alien elite was its protection from legislative attack by its use of the Constitution and, even more, by the ability of the Supreme Court to nullify reform legislation at both the state and national levels. Beard's most important historical treatise, *An Economic Interpretation of the Constitution,* was designed to discredit the Constitution and the Supreme Court by demonstrating the selfish European materialism of the men at Philadelphia and their eager use of European concepts of institutional and hierarchical authority. He assumed that once the people became aware of the alien nature of the Constitution and its conspiratorial use by the capitalist aristocracy, they would rise up in righteous wrath and remove this last major obstacle to the unfettered progress of industrialism.

Beard had argued that industrialism was capable of liberating America because he had seen it working in Germany and England to destroy the last vestiges of medievalism in the Old World. Unlike the American forest, industrialism was an international frontier force. It could liberate men everywhere; on every continent there could be a restored Garden of Eden. Accordingly, when war broke out

in 1914, he saw a feudal aristocracy in Germany as an irrational contradiction to the growth of industrial progress
in that country; a desperate aristocracy was making a last
mad attempt to destroy progress and democracy. Beard
called on the American people to participate in a holy
crusade that would rid the world of the last major obstacle
to international democracy; the feudal remnants must be
crushed by the omnipotent material strength of industrialism. With victory in 1918, he was ready to take the final
step into a national and international paradise.

    Then came 1919 and the end of great expectations. The
irrationalities of international power politics remained
abroad, and economic greed and selfishness were still the
order of the day at home. What had gone wrong? Beard
refused to change his view of human nature. The individual,
he insisted, was still basically good except when corrupted
by institutions and traditions. Did this mean that industrialism was not as powerful as he had once believed, that it was
less capable of freeing the individual from social complexity? Beard confessed that he had overestimated the power
of industrialism. Clearly, it could not melt the almost infinite
layers of the old culture which lay like a monstrous glacier
on Europe, smothering any possibility of a resurgence of
freedom. But he had good news for the citizens of the
United States. If the foundation of Europe was endless
history, here in America the rock on which the nation had
been built was nature. Until 1800, the fundamental reality
of America was the New World Eden. Only a century of
European capitalist corruption, therefore, had submerged
the immutable truths of nature. Surely the force of industrialism could sweep away this alien establishment and
restore the Jeffersonian-Jacksonian covenant. All that was
needed, Beard asserted at the beginning of the 1920's, to
ensure the ultimate rescue of the American saints was a
policy of stern isolation from the rest of the world.

He had returned to the Puritan Jeremiad of Roger Chillingworth. The salvation of the saints depended upon their withdrawal from the sinful brotherhood of mankind. In a fortress America all the temptations of the wicked doctrines of Europe could be excluded by rigid political and economic isolation. The European-oriented eastern aristrocracy must quickly wither and vanish without ideological and economic sustenance from their Old World roots. Then, when this evil class had disappeared, the pure American producers, agrarian and industrial, the simple and good people would live in eternal peace and harmony within their isolated Garden, separated by those great moats, the Atlantic and the Pacific oceans, from the terror of history to which the sinners of the Old World were doomed.

## 1

Not all of Beard's generation were able to salvage even such a limited hope from the collapse of their millennial commitment. No great novelists appeared during the progressive movement to challenge its latter-day version of Bancroft's frontier faith. Nor did any appear during these decades of optimism to give artistic affirmation to Charles Beard's rediscovery of the American Adam.

One novelist of limited aesthetic skill did, however, match Beard's popularity as a public philosopher for the progressive movement. Winston Churchill wrote nine major novels. Five were the best sellers for the years in which they were published. Two were the second best sellers, another was third; only one failed to find a tremendous response from America's middle-class readers. Churchill then is a cultural phenomenon of considerable importance even if he failed to achieve the level of artistic greatness. What we find in his novels is a direct expression of the progressive argument that it was to be 1914, rather than 1828, when history was to end. It was then that men were to be redeemed and made innocent, ready to enter the American Garden.

Churchill had begun to explore the problems of the twentieth century from a perspective much like that of William Dean Howells. In his first political novels, *Coniston* and *Mr. Crewe's Career*, he described the corruption of nineteenth-century America by the doctrine of individual selfishness. He correlated the decline of national morality with the triumph of political democracy and *laissez-faire* capitalism. His villains, like the politician, Jethro Bass, were self-made men who suffered from the delusion that they had no responsibility to the community; they were corrupted by a culture which defined the self-sufficient individual as the only reality. Churchill contrasted these unhappy, driven men with the surviving colonial aristocrats who had a sense of social responsibility and who could achieve personal equilibrium.

In many respects these novels seem almost a reworking of Howells's discovery of society in the 1880's. Churchill, like the older novelist, was not content with the qualified virtue of those vestiges of aristocracy which continued to exist within the wider sea of the middle-class corruption; he was straining to find a way to restore innocence to the land.

By 1913 when he published *The Inside of the Cup*, it was obvious that Churchill had become a convert to progressive millennialism. He was prepared to argue the intellectual possibility of the transcendence of currupt culture by the hidden Adamic personality within each individual. He now rejected all of Howells's doubts about the innate goodness of the individual, and accepted the progressive faith that all evil was from the environment. In making the Reverend John Hodder, an Episcopalian minister, the central figure of his novel, he was able to cancel his own personal commitment to America's nineteenth-century aristocracy. Inevitably the theology of the Reverend Hodder focused on the innate sinfulness of man. The close cultural relationship of his church to the existing aristocratic groups in America made it natural for him to believe in the importance of social structure to restrain the evil in men.

But now Churchill, who had previously defined himself as an aristocrat, an Episcopalian and a patrician reformer, has his hero experience a conversion to the new religious faith of the social gospel. The optimism of this gospel expressed in theological terms the general faith of progressivism, that evil was forced on the individual by the institutions and traditions of society; every individual was inherently good, and if each were to refuse to act according to social standards and instead act according to his instincts, the millennium would occur. Hodder was suddenly brought to see that "God trusted individuals. . . . What did that mean? Individual responsibility! It was as though a searchlight were flung ahead of him and he saw, dimly, a new order—a new order in government and religion."

This new order was possible because God trusted individuals in spite of the record of history which seemed to demonstrate the evil of every man. Beneath the surface "we have a conscious, or lower, human self, and a subconscious, or better self. This subconscious self stretches down, as it were, into the depths of the universe and taps the source of spiritual power. And it is through the subconscious self that every man is potentially divine. Potentially, because the conscious self has to reach out by an effort of the will to effect this union with the spiritual in the subconscious. Apparently from without, as a gift, and therefore in theological language, it is called grace. This is what is meant by being 'born again,' the incarnation of the spirit in the conscious, or human. The two selves are no longer divided, and the higher self assumes control."

*The Inside of the Cup* is in effect an autobiographical novel, in which the author reveals the arguments that converted him to the coming millennium. In his next novel, *A*

*Far Country,* Churchill began to elaborate on his vision. It is interesting to contrast the socialist hero of this book, Hermann Krebs, with Lindau of Howells's *A Hazard of New Fortunes*. Howells had treated Lindau with dignity because he sympathized with his dream of a perfected America, while rejecting Lindau's hope that a violent revolution could establish the dream as reality. Krebs, preaching a gospel of love, believes in the inevitability of the millennium. "The birthright of the spirit of man was freedom, freedom to experiment, to determine, to create—to create himself, to create society in the image of God." No revolutionist, Krebs has the earthly drive and the practical knowledge of a successful business leader.

Churchill's dream of an American Adam in an industrialized Garden was not too far afield from the Jeffersonian arcadia. In an article of 1916, "A Plea for the American Tradition," the author pointed out that the American socialist utopia remained only an escape from Old World history. Unlike European socialism, ours would have no institutionalized framework but would depend only on voluntary association and voluntary cooperation.

When one reads the intellectual biographies of the leading philosophers of progressivism like Charles Beard, one becomes aware of how the experience of World War I smashed their dreams in a way that never happened to the Jacksonians. Certainly every sensitive Jacksonian was aware after the Civil War that something was wrong in the American Garden. But even as perceptive a man as Mark Twain labored throughout his entire lifetime to define the disintegration of the Jeffersonian republic. The prophets of the industrial utopia saw their faith destroyed while they were still young men; their apocalyptic dream suffered an apocalyptic death. They had marched to Armageddon, certain of victory, and the forces of darkness had risen up to annihilate the hosts of the virtuous. For those who had completely dedicated their hearts and their minds to the coming earthly kingdom, 1919 spelled catastrophe. Winston Churchill was one of these.

As he observed the holocaust of war in Europe after 1914, he gradually came to lose his faith in the essential goodness of man. By 1917, when Charles Beard was predicting a world made safe for democracy, this most popular novelist of progressivism had developed grave doubts about the possibility of democracy in the United States. His millennial vision had depended upon the triumph of the innocent individual over corrupt society. In 1917, he published his last novel, *The Dwelling-Place of Light*. He was never to write another; his faith in innocence had perished.

Churchill could not accept Beard's compromise with defeat. There was no chosen people in the New World which could isolate itself from the rest of mankind. The sin of selfishness was the American way of life, of the poor as well as the rich. There was no innocence to preserve, except that of the solitary individual who somehow retained personal virtue in the midst of social corruption. Broken in spirit and mind, Churchill withdrew from this world of chaos and war to survive behind the neutrality of a personal separate peace. He lived out the rest of his life in complete isolation from society, a discredited prophet of peace in a civilization that was arming itself for the next great slaughter.

## 2

What future was there for the sons of the fathers whose prophecy of the millennium had been shattered? What course of action remained meaningful to those whose fathers had retreated from a world which refused to conform to their ideals? The young novelists of the 1920's are commonly described as rebels who exiled themselves from the mainstream of American culture. But in what way did an Ernest Hemingway, for instance, reject Charles Beard and Winston Churchill? Could he not be described, rather, as a loyal and devoted son of these fathers?

Hemingway was a child of Puritans, moreover of defeated Puritans. The grimness of the Hemingway hero is not that of Chillingworth and Ahab; he will make no mad and violent attempt to impose his ideal on the world. He is a young man who has seen his elders march to Armageddon in 1917, dedicated to the destruction of the last vestiges of medieval culture, to the annihilation of every white whale which qualified the perfection of the earth. And he has watched these dispirited warriors straggle homeward, crippled by mortal spiritual wounds.

The youthful Hemingway hero knows that the sons cannot prevail where the fathers have failed, but he is unable to forget their vanquished ideals. Instead he will surrender his own youth and join them in their sterile senility as they live out their hopeless days in nostalgia reminiscing of what might have been.

The Hemingway hero is a simple Deerslayer, suddenly snatched from the spacious security and harmony of the American forest, and forced into the terror of history where peace is replaced by violent death. Overnight, the young and buoyant Deerslayer has become an aged and bitter Leatherstocking awaiting death with fear and trembling on the lifeless prairie. In the experience of World War I, the American frontiersman has learned that he represents a vulnerable myth which cannot conquer culture and lead mankind back into the Garden. But the Hemingway hero, unlike Cooper's Natty Bumppo, does not embrace the civilization which had defeated him. Stubbornly, he will remain loyal to an impotent ideal and so, again unlike Leatherstocking, await his end full of bitterness that the myth has failed.

Hemingway, the child of the middle-class Midwest, was born just in time to be raised in the golden glow of progressivism. His personal experience even came to exaggerate the progressive rediscovery of nature; his suburban family spent its summers amidst the forests and lakes of the Michigan vacation area. He came to know at first hand the redemptive wilderness that the bourgeois vicariously enjoyed. When he graduated from high school, he went to Italy to join the war. Here boyhood romance became the reality. Hemingway was wounded. But for him, it was no red badge of courage; it symbolized a separate peace. The individual must withdraw within himself to find peace because there was none to be found in the world. Unlike Crane's Henry Fleming, he would not turn to face reality and rejoin the army of humanity in its eternal battle; he had received a psychic wound from which he was never to recover and which kept him from reaching maturity. By Crane's values, the young Hemingway was doomed to remain a cowardly boy.

The controlling image of Crane's vision of the universe is complexity, confusion, even nothingness: in Hemingway it is death. What Crane calls bravery, Hemingway pronounces delusion, and what the older writer calls cowardice, Hemingway sees as virtuous self-restraint. Crane demands action; Hemingway affirms the virtue of inaction. The hero of the Lost Generation calls for a courageous confrontation of reality but he refuses to act within the context of that reality. For him, virtue is innocence, courage is impotence, and death is the end.

Hemingway's first book, *In Our Time,* opens with a scene the author had experienced as a reporter after World War I in the evacuation of Turkey by Greek civilians. Two images emerge. One is the horror of birth, how the women "screamed every night at midnight." The other is the terror of death, "The worst . . . were the women with dead babies. You couldn't get the women to give up their dead babies." This alien scene is followed directly by the story, "Indian Camp." Hemingway's autobiographical Nick Adams is going with his doctor father to witness the birth of a baby. Here is the paradise of the Michigan wilderness, and the mother and father are Indians, the children of nature. This is not Smyrna, not the terror of Old World history; this is the American Garden. Surely here life is not the terror of birth and death.

When Nick comes to the Indian cabin, the mother is in extreme pain. She is unable to have the baby naturally, and Nick's father must perform a Cesarean section. In childbirth, this most fundamental of all human experiences, the youthful Nick finds no beauty and dignity, no joy. When the birth is completed, the doctor turns to the upper bunk where the father of the child is lying. "He pulled back the blanket from the Indian's head. His hand came away wet. He mounted on the edge of the lower bunk with a lamp in one hand and looked in. The Indian lay with his face toward the wall. His throat had been cut from ear to ear . . . Nick, standing in the door of the kitchen, had a good view of the upper bunk when his father, the lamp in one hand, tipped the Indian's head back."

Nowhere can life escape from death; existence is a meaningless tragedy. The remaining short stories of *In Our Time* repeat the same theme. Nick Adams never loses his commitment to innocence. Each story, each experience repeats the shock of discovery that dreams are not to be realized in this world.

He is initiated into the reality of the family through observing his mother and father. His mother has retreated from a loveless marriage to her room, there to seek consolation in Christian Science. His father has retreated to the woods to be consoled by hunting. At the center of the family there is only a great void. Rather than face such a life of mechanical pretense, Nick breaks off his affair with the girl he loves. Already old beyond his years, he knows the emotion cannot last. Nothing is permanent, not even comradeship with his friend, Bill. Their interest in baseball, in books, in drinking, even in hunting, has no intrinsic value. Like their conversation, these interests are mechanically developed to fill the void.

When Nick Adams runs away from this monumental failure of middle-class innocence in search of a better world, he meets up with the Battler, a hobo and one-time boxer whose features have been beaten into a grotesque parody of the human form, and who would destroy Nick for no reason other than that his mind is as distorted as his face. The Battler's Negro companion coolly and tenderly renders him insensible with a blackjack, explaining that this restores him to sanity. So much for Nick's encounter with the heroic natural man.

From America he goes to Europe and its war. And Europe only confirms his adolescent experiences of the lack of meaning in human existence where ideals always are doomed. The single paragraph scenes from Nick's experience in the war, which separate and bind the short stories, now reach a culmination. Each has been a scene of equally meaningless violence. Now it is Nick who "sat against the wall of the church where they had dragged him to be clear of machine gun fire. Both legs stuck out awkwardly. He had been hit in the spine . . . Rinaldi, big-backed, his equipment sprawling, lay face downward against the wall . . . Nick turned his head and looked down at Rinaldi. 'Senta Rinaldi, Senta you and me, we've made a separate peace.'"

Nick Adams and Ernest Hemingway had made their separate peace in Europe. It was the wounds of the European war, physical and emotional, which had brought them finally to accept the meaning of all their adolescent experience—that there was no meaning. All cultural values were shams. Becoming expatriates from America, they would spend their remaining years in Europe without roots in either continent.

In the story, "Soldier's Home," Hemingway outlined the necessity for his exile. Krebs went to the war from a Methodist College in Kansas, and at Belleau Wood, Soissons, and in the Argonne, he had learned that the American promise of innocence was a lie. He came home alienated from his father, who believed in the value of a business career, and from his mother, who believed in the existence of innocence. The girls of the town "were too complicated . . . He did not want to get into the intrigue and the politics. He did not want to have to do any courting. He did not want to tell any more lies. It wasn't worth it. He did not want any consequences. He did not want any consequences ever again. He wanted to live along without consequences. He would go to live in Europe where he would be free of consequences."

If there is irony in the need for the American to live in exile in Europe where his hope for the earthy fulfillment of his dream of innocence was completely shattered, there is even greater irony in his refusal to surrender the dream. He remains loyal to the ideal of innocence he learned from those middle-class parents whom he has so bitterly rejected. If the first story of *In Our Time*, "Indian Camp," begins Nick Adams's alienation from the myth of redemptive nature, the last story, "Big Two-Hearted River," brings him back to the scenes of his childhood in Michigan fruitlessly to repeat rituals which are intended to bring him into harmony with nature. And so adult Nick Adams, repatriated, sets off on a solitary fishing trip in the scenes of his childhood. When he descends from the train, however, he notices that the town was gone, the landscape black and barren. "The country was burned over and changed, but it did not matter. It could not all be burned."

Desperately, Nick Adams wants to believe that "It could not all be burned," that he can still re-create the innocence of his childhood. Momentarily, he would escape the terror of history by pretending that he was a child, living in "space as spaciousness," capable of "total possibility." He marches through the ashes of the countryside until he reaches the river, and there he makes his camp. "He was settled. Nothing could touch him. It was a good place to camp. He was there, in the good place. He was in his home where he had made it."

Emerging from his tent the next morning, Nick is content with the ritual of camping, the ritual of play which has replaced all concern with the outside world. Concentrating on the techniques of fishing he can escape from the world. "Nick felt awkward and professionally happy with all his equipment hanging from him. . . . He stepped into the stream. It was a shock. His trousers clung tight to his legs. His shoes felt the gravel. The water was a rising cold shock.

"Rushing, the current sucked against his legs. When he stepped in, the water was over his knees. He waded with the current. The gravel slipped under his shoes. . . . Now the water deepened up his thighs sharply and coldly. Ahead was the smooth dammed-back flood of water above the logs. The water was smooth and dark; on the left, the lower edge of the meadow; on the right, the swamp.

"Ahead the river narrowed and went into a swamp. The river became smooth and deep and the swamp looked solid with cedar trees, their trunks close together, their branches solid. . . .

"Nick did not want to go in there now. . . . In the swamp fishing was a tragic adventure. Nick did not want it."

For Hemingway, as for Mark Twain, the river was the last refuge for the dream of innocence in the valley of democracy. But this river could no more wash away Nick's experience with violence and evil than the Mississippi itself could lift Huck Finn out of the horrors that occurred on its shores. Huck Finn had learned that his beloved river was two-hearted. It promised salvation but delivered him back into evil. Nick Adams could learn no less.

For Hemingway, the only way to preserve human dignity in the swamp of existence was to refuse to participate in the futile attempts of man to impose values and

order on the indifferent universe. In his hatred of historical
society, he remained true to his Puritan heritage. Civilization
seduced man into believing he could achieve fulfillment,
only to frustrate him in the end. By resisting the temptation
of culture, one could achieve a kind of innocence, but one
which was tragically impotent. Jake Barnes, the hero of
Hemingway's first novel, *The Sun Also Rises,* is the representative of such a philosophy. He is invulnerable because
he is impotent. Since he cannot bring about the consum-
mation of his love for Lady Brett, he is spared from disil-
lusion; his incapacity saves him from the wheel of time
which crushes all human pretentions. He can keep his love
for a woman timeless, untouched by the corruption of the
flesh.

At the end of the novel, when Lady Brett exclaims,
"Oh, Jake . . . we could have had such a damned good
time together," he replies, "Yes . . . isn't it pretty to think
so?" He knows that the dream of perfection can never be
fulfilled. In his self-conscious pose as a realistic coward,
Jake is filled with a sense of guilt. Again and again he feels
the need to explain why he has made his separate peace.
This compulsive theme of self-explanation continues in *A
Farewell to Arms.*

Lt. Frederick Henry had always been "embarrassed by
the words sacred, glorious and sacrifice," but he had never
questioned his own loyalty to the army—until the retreat at
Caparetto. As he sees the army disintegrate, the young
American senses the meaninglessness of the war. He wants
out. He wants to "forget the war," for he, too, "had made a
separate peace."

In Switzerland he renews his idyll with Catherine, who
is in the last months of her pregnancy. Significantly, this
interlude takes place in the timelessness of winter, whereas
their first ecstasy had been in the timefulness of summer.
Now it is spring, and they await the birth of their child,
while the snows of winter are melting and earth prepares

for its regeneration. The baby dies, and Frederick Henry knows that "Now Catherine would die. That was what you did. You died . . . You could count on that. Stay around and they would kill you." The universe was as hostile to the individual as it was to society. "It kills the very good and the very gentle and the very brave impartially. If you are none of these you can be sure it will kill you too but there will be no special hurry." Life begins with suffering and ends in death. Hemingway had witnessed the first in Michigan with young Nick Adams. He saw it again in Italy with a mature Frederick Henry. There was no escape from reality.

It is perhaps not too imaginative to hear him cry out to Melville's Ahab for forgiveness because he does not have the courage to continue the struggle. Like Nick and Frederick, he had been wounded too desperately to renew the battle against the implacable force of the universe. Ahab sought out death in his vain ambition to conquer it, and Hemingway, the child of Ahab, remains loyal to the father's vision although he knows from the fate of the elder that the dream of perfection can never be fulfilled. All he can do is preserve the dream in his own heart by surviving as an impotent innocent. As long as he lives, he will remain a Puritan.

# 3

F. Scott Fitzgerald's *The Geat Gatsby,* published in 1925, stands directly in the tradition of *The Scarlet Letter, Moby-Dick,* and *The American.* It also foreshadows the writings of William Faulkner and Robert Penn Warren of the 1930's and 1940's. Fitzgerald sensed that the myth of the American Adam and the American Eden was bankrupt, had indeed always been morally indefensible, even though he was unable to find another faith to live by. *The Great Gatsby* is truly a document of the Lost Generation. It is self-criticism without constructive purpose. It destroys the hidden and isolated refuge of Ernest Hemingway without offering the promise of a fruitful reunion with humanity.

When we see that there is a significant thematic parallel between *The Great Gatsby* and *Moby-Dick,* we are able to understand more fully why Hemingway despised and feared Fitzgerald as a romantic who lacked the courage to live by the puritanical code. The two major figures in *The Great Gatsby* are Nick Carraway, apparently the man of complete self-restraint, and Jay Gatsby, the man of no self-restraint. Fitzgerald, by illuminating the emotional hold that Gatsby has on Carraway, makes a devastating commentary on the burden of guilt which Hemingway carried because he had deserted Ahab's quest for timeless perfection.

Nick Carraway, like a Hemingway hero, sees himself as free from the burden of culture, able to live directly with and by the facts of experience, without the illusions and myths which tormented the bourgeoisie; he represents the relationship of the expatriate to the middle-class imagination. Europeans had fled the Old World to escape its corruption and to find innocence, to escape timefulness and to find timelessness. These middle-class people believed that innocence was possible if man turned away from the false theories of medieval civilization to live by the concrete facts of experience. To Fitzgerald, this was only the appearance of a pragmatic or empirical outlook. In reality, it was a platonic philosophy; it assumed the perfect organic expression of the ideal in material form. For the European bourgeois coming to the New World, the ideal expressed itself in two major material forms—the American landscape and money. As Fitzgerald presents the career of Nick Carraway, he is posing an embarrassing question for the Lost Generation: What is the essential difference between the innocence of Nick Carraway, the expatriate, and that of the American middle class?

Nick is a young, tough, sophisticated observer as dedicated as Jake Barnes to a life without illusions. The son of an established midwestern family, graduated from Yale in 1915, he had gone to war in 1917, and has come home to his native citadel of the American Garden with his faith in the millennium destroyed. "I came back restless," he says. "Instead of being the warm center of the world, the Middle West now seemed like the ragged edge of the universe—so I decided to go East and learn the bond business."

Nick Carraway, like the Hemingway expatriates, goes into exile from his home, where the ideal of organic perfection has failed. He will live in the East where there are no illusions and where friendship is on the factual basis of money. Expelled from the Garden, he wants us to believe that he has no moral commitments, no set of values by which he judges the world. "I'm inclined to reserve all judgments," he declares, trying to persuade us that he is the absolutely neutral observer. "I am one of the few honest people that I have ever known."

Faced with the collapse of the hope of the good society where every citizen is a saint, Nick Carraway, like Hemingway, continues to declare that goodness is still the social norm. He knows there is no fulfillment of innocence in society; only the individual can save his personal integrity. Is not this ideal of personal innocence outside of traditional society the one which motivated Europeans when they fled from the east to the west? This ideal of friendship solidly based on the material values of the market place was the ideal of the European bourgeois as they came from the Old World to the New. And is not this then the continuing American middle-class definition of the good society: a mechanical arrangement of self-sufficient individuals, each able to pay his own way, and therefore innocent?

For Fitzgerald, there was no Europe and no America, there was no East and no West. There were only hypocrites who pretended that innocence was to be found in America and not in Europe, or in the West and not in the East, or in some individuals and not in others, who disguised their selfishness behind the mark of puritan saintliness. Nick Carraway was such a puritan saint. The prisoner of anarchistic bourgeois ideology, he is incapable of any fruitful human relationships. He fulfills all the stereotypes of Henry James's *The American.*

Like the American, he sensed the inadequacy of the abstractions which supposedly defined life in the West; he wanted only that life in the East which could be bought. Never would he surrender his independence, his self-sufficiency. In New York City, he lives a life of almost total alienation. It is true that briefly he has an "affair with a girl who lived in Jersey City and worked in the accounting department, but her brother began throwing mean looks in my direction, so when she went on her vacation in July, I let it blow quietly away." With proper self-restraint, there need never be any consequences.

Nick, the alienated American, who works in the city but lives in the suburbs, denies a meaningful relationship between his work and his home. He passes each day through a "valley of ashes." This sterile desert is the vital connecting link between the American's self-image as a man of spirituality and the reality of his materialism.

In the lush beauty of West Egg and East Egg, Long Island, described by Fitzgerald in caressing details which render them as lifeless and false as a movie set, Nick becomes reacquainted with a distant cousin, Daisy Buchanan, who is married to an immensely wealthy man. Tom Buchanan and Daisy are both from the Midwest. For Fitzgerald, every American is from the Midwest because that is where the dream of perfection was to be fulfilled. Now in the 1920's, they have been expelled from the Garden that never was to live in the reality of the wasteland of the East. There is no happiness for these bankrupts of the American dream. They have discovered that money cannot buy fulfillment, but they cannot escape their commitment to money because they cannot escape their commitment to self-sufficiency. Tom and Daisy live as strangers in the same house. They are bored, frustrated, restless, without hope.

Nick Carraway is attracted to Jordan Baker, the female counterpart of himself, whose "bored, haughty face" must match his own. When he remembers that she was once involved in a minor scandal he feels relieved. He can continue to consider himself the last honest person, who is free to judge without ever being judged. Meanwhile he can begin a relationship with Jordan telling himself that "it makes no difference to me" that she is dishonest. Of course, it makes every difference because now he need have no concern for consequences.

For some time, Nick had been filled with curiosity about this neighbor who staged elaborate parties and was reputed to be a bootlegger and a killer. When he finally meets the mysterious Gatsby he finds a gentle-looking young man who speaks with an affected accent and relates a personal history so grotesque, so patently a tissue of lies as to take on the proportions of an inspired fantasy. Suddenly for Nick, the self-styled cynical observer, "It was all true. I saw the skins of tigers flaming in his palace on the Grand Canal: I saw him opening a chest of rubies." Nick can sympathize with Gatsby, who wants to impose his ideals on reality; can vicariously share his mad effort to make the world conform to his vision of perfection. He is not too surprised when Gatsby asks him to bring Daisy to his house, even offers him money to arrange a meeting; he is only mildly embarrassed by Gatsby's offer to buy his services as a high-class pimp. In fact he rejoices that here is an American who still believes in the possibility of the unity of the ideal and the real. Gatsby still believes that man can bring the spiritual and the material into timeless harmony. For him, Daisy is the earthly symbol of this possibility.

He had once been in love with her before Tom

Buchanan had married her. Now he plans to win her back—
by proving that he is more dedicated to American materialism than her husband is. And so he parades the immensity
of his house, the luxury of his furnishings, the enormousness
of his parties before Daisy. She will never be alone, he
promises, because he can afford to keep his house "always
full of interesting people, night and day. People who do
interesting things. Celebrated people."

This high priest of materialism asks Daisy to compare
her husband's tasteless consumption of expensive clothes
with his own careful choice of vestments. He comes to her
"in a white flannel suit, silver shirt, and gold-colored tie."
He takes her to his wardrobe where "he took out a pile of
shirts and began throwing them, one by one before us, shirts
of sheer linen and thick silk and white flannel, which lost
their folds as they fell and covered the table in many-
colored disarray . . . Suddenly with a strained sound, Daisy
bent her head into the shirts and began to cry stormily.

" 'They're such beautiful shirts,' she sobbed."

The American Adam knows the way to win the heart
of the American Eve whose voice "was full of money—that
was the inexhaustible charm that rose and fell in it."

Now Fitzgerald's satire has reached its most dramatic
moment of barbed criticism. He will strip from Gatsby, the
American Adam, these multiple layers of luxurious disguise,
to reveal the direct descendant of Roger Chillingworth,
Captain Ahab, and the Princess Casamassima. Here in this
holy of holies, a phone rings. Gatsby answers, "Yes . . .
Well, I can't talk now . . . I can't talk now, old sport. . . .
I said a small town . .   He must know what a small town
is. . . . Well, he's no use to us if Detroit is his idea of a
small town."

This is the great Gatsby, big-time bootlegger and inci-
dental killer of those who imperil his source of wealth—the
American Adam who stands apart from humanity and refuses to be restrained by the human condition. This is

Captain Ahab searching for the limitless power which will
enable him to transcend time and, therefore, death. Nick,
parasitically dependent upon Gatsby's vitality, calls this
man a saint. There is wonderful irony in Nick's harsh criticism of Tom Buchanan's abstract hostility against unknown
enemies and the bland way in which he ignores Gatsby's
real violence against particular individuals.

James Gatz had come off an unsuccessful North Dakota
farm determined to become a self-made man. Since there
was no further frontier of opportunity in the West, he had
to turn back to the East to find the main chance. He came
East, as his ancestors had come West, with a desire to become a new man. His future sprang "from his platonic
conception of himself." As the European immigrants were
symbolically washed clean in crossing the Atlantic, James
Gatz was baptized anew in crossing Lake Superior. The
Europeans had found the miracle of natural treasures in the
New World. James Gatz was discovered by a millionaire
yachting on the lake and started on his way up; an orphan
hero, christened by his own imagination, he was reborn, Jay
Gatsby.

When he met Daisy in 1917 his vision was that she
should be his Eve and together they should live in timeless
harmony in the American Garden. But the war intervened
and Gatsby should have learned from this experience what
Nick understood so well—that there was no innocence, there
was no Eve, no Eden. For Gatsby, however, the timeful
events of the war were only a challenge to his platonic will.
He would bring Daisy back to 1917. He would obliterate
her marriage and her motherhood. He would restore her
virginity. He was not content, therefore, to have Daisy as
a mistress. He must demand that she deny every moment
she had spent with Tom. "He wanted nothing less of Daisy
than that she should go to Tom and say, 'I never loved
you.'"

One hot summer day Nick and Jordan, Gatsby, Daisy

and Tom are all together in the Buchanan house. Daisy has made it clear that she is Gatsby's girl. Tempers are strained, and they decide to drive into the city to pass away the time. Again they drive through the "valley of ashes." For these rootless Americans, alienated from humanity, this wasteland is the true American Garden. In Manhattan, they rent a hotel room and quarrel. Gatsby shouts at Tom that the past five years never existed. " 'She never loved you, do you hear?' he cried. 'She only married you because I was poor and she was tired of waiting for me. It was a terrible mistake, but in her heart she never loved anyone except me.' "

"Oh, you want too much," Daisy cries. "I can't help what's past. . . . I did love him once—but I loved you too."

This qualification of the ideal and the real marks the end of an American dream for the great Gatsby. He could possess Daisy in her timefulness as the eternal woman but he could not have a timeless New World Eve. Defeated by the inevitable imperfection of reality, Gatsby is ready for death. And death comes by chance, which also undermines every attempt to define the world in platonic terms.

Gatsby is buried in the East by his father who, with Nick, is his only mourner. The father has decided that his son should be buried in this alien land because it was on this frontier that he became a success. Like Nick, the defeated young man, this defeated old man respects the puritan vision of self-creation which drove his son away from home. With Gatsby buried, Nick retreats from the chaotic East back to the idyllic Midwest of his childhood memories. "I felt," he declared, "that I wanted the world to be uniform and at a sort of moral attention forever. I wanted no more riotous excursions with privileged glimpses into the human heart." Since, at the beginning of the novel, he had explained his expatriation in the East because "instead of being the warm center of the world, the Middle West now seemed like the ragged edge of the universe," we must conclude that his capacity for self-delusion has only been increased by the events he has observed.

Yet Nick has learned that the East is where the West began, that Europeans sighted Long Island first. "Its vanished trees, the trees that had made way for Gatsby's house, had once pandered in whispers to the last and greatest of all human dreams; for a transitory enchanted moment man must have held his breath in the presence of this continent compelled into an aesthetic contemplation he neither understood nor desired, face to face for the last time in history with something commensurate to his capacity for wonder."

Nick knew that this dream had not found fulfillment and never could. But like Fitzgerald, he cannot imagine an alternative to this "greatest of all human dreams." Stoically, he accepts the burden of innocence which dooms him to the hypocrisy and sterility of the Lost Generation. He can see no other future but that which "year by year recedes before us. . . . So we beat on boats against the current, borne back ceaselessly into the past."

# V

---

# AFTER THE LOST
# GENERATION

---

*William Faulkner*
*Robert Penn Warren*
*James Gould Cozzens*

# 1

At the end of the 1920's William Faulkner suddenly ceased to be a member of the Lost Generation. His angle of vision shifted radically. It changed from that of the individual who considers himself a victim of society because he cannot live a life of innocence, to that of the individual who is victimized by a society that has taught him to strive for innocence. Faulkner made an imaginative leap in which he was no longer to accept the image of the self-exiled individual who has chosen alienation as the most important element in his artistic universe. In his later years, he was to work with the vision of a twisted society that created alienated individuals as the fundamental reality which the novelist must analyze and describe.

When his first novels appeared in the 1920's, they seemed to be inferior copies of those of Hemingway and Fitzgerald. Faulkner too was obsessed by the wound received by the innocent in World War I. His first novel,

*Soldier's Pay*, is the story of Donald Mahon, who left rural Georgia to go to war and is sent home mortally wounded. His fiancée rejects him as already dead, but before he dies a young war widow marries him. Widowed again, Margaret Powers refuses to marry another man whom she loves. Her experience, she says, is that love is always followed by death. She does not have the strength to accept further tragedy.

After writing a satire about the empty sophistication of a group of Lost Generation pseudointellectuals in *Mosquitoes*, Faulkner returned once more to the mortal wound of World War I in *Sartoris*. Young Bayard Sartoris has come back from the war without a purpose in life: "His head was clear and cold; the whiskey he had drunk was completely dead. Or rather, it was as though his head were one Bayard who lay on a strange bed and whose alcohol-dulled nerves radiated like threads of ice through that body which he must drag forever about a bleak and barren world with him. 'Hell,' he said, lying on his back, staring out the window where nothing was to be seen, waiting for sleep, not knowing if it would come or not, not caring a particular damn either way." Searching for an honorable way to commit suicide, he succeeds when he takes an unsafe airplane for a test flight.

*Soldier's Pay* and *Sartoris* repeat the assumptions on which Fitzgerald and Hemingway built their philosophy of alienation. They postulate an innocent individual, perfect in his simplicity, whose innate spirituality is threatened by a corrupt and complex society. The American social establishment promised the individual in 1917 that it was dedicated to the creation of an earthly paradise and asked the individual to participate in helping to build the good society. But the promise of paradise became the nightmare of war. The individual realized that he had been seduced by the false promises of a community which would always be both complex and corrupt. Frustrated, he draws back from this profane body to preserve the innocence of his sacred person. Such withdrawal must, of course, lead to the martyrdom of death or impotence. But the idealistic individual preferred martyrdom to compromise; it was better to be lost in alienation than corruption.

Then in 1929, Faulkner published *The Sound and the Fury*, which dramatically rejected this perspective of the alienated individual who withdraws from the world which has failed him. The very structure of the novel symbolizes Faulkner's radically new outlook. He is dealing with a family, not an individual, and he describes the history of the family through the eyes of an idiot, Benjy; a neurotic on the verge of suicide, Quentin; a viciously selfish storekeeper, Jason; and a troubled adolescent girl.

Faulkner makes three major points which separate him from the perspective of the Lost Generation. He asserts the social nature of the individual, his dependence on other individuals. He asserts the existence of psychological depths and weaknesses within each individual. And he asserts the universality of alienation within the Compson family. Alienation is no longer the chosen prerogative of the aristocratic elite known as the Lost Generation. Instead, it is the forced burden of the ordinary individual. Each member of the family is led to tragedy because each believes in his own innocence and selfishly attempts to protect it from violation.

Working furiously with his new vision, Faulkner quickly published *As I Lay Dying*. The Bundrens are a poor-white family. They are not the decayed aristocracy represented by the Compsons, but their spiritual sickness is just as great. As Faulkner reveals the reactions of the husband and children to the death of the mother, he describes individuals who are moral monsters, incapable of sacrificing themselves for another. Love has no meaning in the lives of those who assume their spiritual self-sufficiency.

In these two novels, Faulkner has come full circle to present the alienated individual, not as an innocent victim but as a destructive being. He suggests that society is not a complex and corrupt entity which threatens the autonomy of the individual, but a wicked environment which teaches the individual the philosophy of selfish alienation, that it is his birthright to be autonomous and innocent and, therefore, self-centered and destructive.

Faulkner's discovery that alienation is pathetic rather than tragic reaches culmination in *Sanctuary,* the third novel he had written within two years. If the Compsons and the Bundrens, the Southern aristocracy and the Southern poor-whites, refused to treat one another with love, if they were self-centered and defensive of their supposed innocence, and incapable of human relationships except in terms of self-interest, why should Faulkner not describe Southern society in terms of a house of prostitution where love is merely a monetary and physical transaction?

While we have no explicit statement by Faulkner of the philosophical relation of these three novels to his earlier three, we can see that he has made a fantastic imaginative leap from the self-pitying, alienated heroes of his Lost Generation fiction to the self-pitying and alienated monsters who are the Compsons and the Bundrens, and the Temple Drake and Popeye of *Sanctuary.* Faulkner had rediscovered Henry James's ironic assertion that the individual is never more the prisoner of society than when he defines himself as an autonomous and self-sufficient atom of innocent self-interest.

The momentum of his journey away from the perspective of the Lost Generation led Faulkner now to the question: What was the crucial factor in Southern society which shaped its members in the direction of alienation? The answer is found in his next novel, *Light in August,* one of the great allegories of American literature. The answer is Puritanism, a national, even international, as well as Southern Puritanism, which has taught men to seek salvation in their own innocence and self-interest rather than as loving and self-sacrificing members of the sinful brotherhood of mankind.

Faulkner had now also rediscovered Hawthorne's insight into the parent source of the ideology of American alienation. Hawthorne had warned Americans that they could become sterile and hate-filled devils like Roger Chillingworth if they accepted the theology of perfection, and Faulkner recognizes his own membership in a community which, for a century, had committed itself to just such a theology. *Light in August* is a retelling of *The Scarlet Letter*. But it is allegorical history, not an allegorical warning. The symbol of the alienated man become devil—Joe Christmas— is central to the story. Roger Chillingworth does not lurk in the forest attempting to corrupt the heart of Arthur Dimmesdale. Inhuman theology and the human heart have become organically intertwined in a living monster who represents the South as it tragically exists.

The story begins with a young country girl from Alabama walking the dust-filled roads which lead to Mississippi. Lena Grove is alone and pregnant. An orphan, living with her brother's family, she has been seduced by a young man who left her with the promise that he will send for her when he gets established in a good job. Lucas Burch, however, has fled west out of Alabama with only one thought— to escape responsibility. Now as Lena plods west through the dust, she is isolated by the failure of Burch to protect her with his love and by the failure of her brother to forgive her sin. The puritan society has exploited her body and denied her spirit.

In dramatic opposition to Jay Gatsby's impossible vision of Daisy as perfect innocence, Faulkner has evoked Lena Grove as a symbol of life in which the ideal must express itself in the mortification of the flesh. Denying the inevitability of human imperfection, the Southern Puritan hates Lena Grove for carrying that new life which symbolizes the continuing imperfection of humanity. Southern society suffers from the sin of pride; seeing themselves as worldly angels, these people have become worldly devils. Here, at the beginning of the novel, Faulkner has begun to create the framework for a Christian allegory. He is offering Southerners the possibility of redemption from their nightmare world of alienation if they accept this fallen woman and her child with love, and are able to identify their fate with Lena Grove and her baby.

As Lena Grove comes into Jefferson, Mississippi, where Burch is living, the town is caught up in great excitement. A house on the outskirts is burning. It belongs to a stranger from the North, Joanna Burden, whose grandfather came to Jefferson during Reconstruction to help the Negro. This Yankee woman is the last of a family that has lived in the South for three generations without being a part of it. Now rushing to the blazing house, the townspeople discover that she has been murdered. Soon they learn that her murderer is the drifter, Joe Christmas.

Christmas had wandered into Jefferson in the recent past and had gone to work at the sawmill until his bootlegging became so profitable that he could devote his full time to his illegal vocation. He had lived in an abandoned shack on Joanna Burden's land with Burch, another stranger who had gone to work at the sawmill. Now Burch is found drunk at the dead woman's house and is held for suspicion of murder. Shocked into sobriety, he shouts his innocence and names his partner, Christmas, as the murderer. The people are quickly persuaded of Burch's innocence when they are told that Christmas is a Negro who has passed as white. This "nigger" has killed and probably raped a white woman. Blind fury generates a lynch mob, and the hunt is on.

Ultimately, they will find Joe Christmas because, when he runs away, he is actually running toward capture and death; the path to destruction is the one Christmas, the alienated man, must choose to fulfill the meaning of his life.

"He never acted like either a nigger or a white man. That was it. That was what made the folks so mad."

The story of Joe Christmas is the center of the novel, and its structure reveals the reason he cut Joanna Burden's throat and now waits in nearby Mottstown to be captured. The circle that starts from the murder to probe his history and returns to his execution is intimately related to the history of Lena Groves's unborn child. Will her child have the same history as Joe Christmas? When Faulkner poses this possibility, we remember that we are dealing with a Christian allegory whose chief protagonist is Southern society. Will this society accept with love a child born in sin? If it does not, then it must continue to suffer alienation and death. Since the history of Joe Christmas is also one of alienation and death, we must consider him the symbolic representative of the puritanical South itself.

Like Lena Groves's unborn child, Joe is illegitimate; his mother ran away with a man from a passing carnival. Her father, Doc Hines, pursued them and killed the man, then imprisoned his daughter in his house and denied her medical attention while he waited for the child to be born. After she dies in childbirth, he takes his grandson to a distant orphanage.

What is the motivation of Doc Hines in these monstrous acts? Faulkner explains him as a Puritan who assumes the possibility of a sinless existence in this world. When his daughter sins, he cannot forgive her. She must be punished, the sin itself must be punished, and Doc Hines will serve as God's agent. His actions are those of a righteous God of wrath.

Faulkner defines the place of the Negro in this Puritan imagination. Unwilling to accept responsibility for their own imperfections, the whites had found a scapegoat for their fear and hatred in the Negro. The Negro, that black offspring of the devil, has defiled the Southern Garden. That is why Hines, self-appointed agent of the Lord to defend the virtue of the white race against the evil of the black, declares his daughter's seducer was a Negro. The child of sin who is therefore tainted by blackness must be punished.

This idea is firmly fixed in Joe Christmas when he blunders into a sexual adventure of the orphanage's dietitian. Anxious to get the boy out of the institution before he can reveal her secret, she learns from Hines that Joe is a Negro, and rushes to her superiors with the news. To avoid any scandalous revelation of their mistake, Joe is put out for adoption with a childless farm couple, the McEacherns, who take the boy assuming that he is white. McEachern is a stern Puritan who demands rigid religious orthodoxy from his adopted son, and when Joe refuses, punishes him severely. But Joe seeks out this punishment. Believing himself to be a Negro passing as the child of white parents, he is overcome with guilt and searches for all the punishment the white man will give him.

For the same reason that he welcomes Mr. McEachern's beatings, he must violently reject Mrs. McEachern's love. How monstrous it would be if he allowed this white woman to shower her affections on the black blood which was masquerading within his white skin. Joe fears Mrs. McEachern because he is tempted to accept her love. He begins to wander aimlessly across the face of the nation, totally alienated from himself and from every living person. Joe is not only white, he thinks like a white man. He hates the Negroes who have robbed him of his right to innocence and avoids contact with them.

Eventually, having arrived at the age when Christ died, he comes to Jefferson, Mississippi, and takes a job in a sawmill. Passing as a white, he keeps himself aloof from the town in an unused shack on Joanna Burden's land. Here, this upholder of Southern white mores, a hater of Yankee "nigger-lovers," he conceives a great revenge. The Negroes, befriended by this Yankee woman, have never turned against her, but Joe Christmas has it in his power to make a Negro violate her trust. He rapes her.

She disappoints him, however, by accepting his violence. Joanna's father has taught her that all Yankees have the burden of caring for the Negro because God has made this burden "the curse of every white child that was ever born and that ever will be born. None can escape it." She must help the Negroes not because they are brothers to be loved but because they are animals that God has placed within the American Eden to be cared for. Like Christmas, then, she expects the Negro to act like a beast and, at last, one has.

For Faulkner, there is no difference between Northern and Southern puritanism. Joanna Burden, behind her facade of Christian respectability, is the same kind of moral monstrosity as Doc Hines. When she is raped, she enjoys this experience of brute sex without love. She might have been appalled had Joe been a white man but when he tries to shock her by revealing his Negro identity, she is enraptured. She, who has been taught to see Negroes "not as a people, but as a thing, a shadow in which I lived," has always expected this thing to turn on her. Now that it has, she is glad. For months, she takes Joe nightly as her lover or rather she repeats the ritual of her original rape, as she shouts in ecstasy, "Negro! Negro! Negro!"

It is his sin, not hers, and she descends into the depths of degradation. When the thrill of sin wanes, she must think of regulating and moralizing this relationship. She must be responsible for the Negro even to the point of so humbling herself that she will marry him. Christmas has raped her but she will uplift him. She tells Joe that he will marry her and share her responsibilities of caring for the Negro community.

Joe has tolerated these months of orgiastic sex because, as a Southern white, he has enjoyed the continuing degradation of the Yankee spinster. He has defined himself as a Negro only during the sexual act and then only to break her pride. Now suddenly, she is asking him to become a public Negro, to go to a Negro college to train himself to work with Negroes as brothers. It is the ultimate outrage to this Southern white. "To school," he shouted, "A nigger school. Me . . . And then learn law in the office of a nigger lawyer . . . Tell niggers that I am a nigger too?"

For Joanna Burden, it has become an absolute necessity that Joe Christmas accept his identity as a Negro; it is the only way that she can escape the responsibility of sin in their continuing sexual relationship. But Joe refuses her last plea, she plans to shoot him and commit suicide. Her ancient pistol misfires and Joe murders her.

Joanna Burden had failed to understand that Christmas never thought of himself as a Negro, that he had always seen himself as a white polluted by the black blood in his veins. Brilliantly, Faulkner evokes the madness that was growing in Christmas during the last days of his relationship with Joanna when he describes Joe's walk through the Negro district of Jefferson: "As from the bottom of a thick black pit he saw himself enclosed by cabin shapes, vague, kerosenelit, so that the street lamps themselves seemed to be farther spaced, as if the black life, the black breathing had compounded the substance of breath. . . . He began to run, glaring, his teeth glaring . . . a narrow and rutted lane turned and mounted . . . out of the black hollow. . . . Then he became cool. The Negro smell, the Negro voices were behind and below him."

Joe Christmas kills Joanna Burden because she threatens to push him back down into this black pit. But in murdering this white woman, he has sealed his doom as a Negro and fallen irretrievably into the black depths of Negro existence. He has committed the worst crime a Negro can perpetrate, the rape and murder of a white woman. As a white man, he has the responsibility of seeing that the black blood within him is punished. "He could see himself being hunted by white men at last into the black abyss which had been waiting, trying, for thirty years to drown him and into which now and at last he had actually entered." The white Joe Christmas will throw himself into the abyss to gain revenge against the black Joe Christmas. He must capture himself if as a white man he is to achieve any dignity in this disaster.

Joe goes to Mottstown to await his fate. This is the completion of his circle; he has returned to his maker, his grandfather, Doc Hines, who lives here and travels around the countryside preaching white supremacy to intimidated congregations in Negro churches. When Doc hears that the "nigger" killer from Jefferson has been caught, he rushes to organize a lynch mob, shouting, "kill the bastard!"

If Joanna Burden is the symbolic representative of the North's relation to Southern history, Gail Hightower represents the Southern aristocracy which had failed to provide responsible leadership in the generations after the Civil War. The only child of an elderly Puritan, Hightower as a young man had dedicated himself to the memory of his romantic grandfather who had fought so gallantly in the war and was killed in a raid on Jefferson. Hightower had entered the ministry with but one thought—to get a pulpit in Jefferson. "It was the town he desired to live in and not the church . . . he did not care about the people, the living people." And when he preached, "it was as if he couldn't get religion and the galloping cavalry and his dead grandfather shot from the galloping horse untangled from each other, even in the pulpit."

He was as irresponsible in his obligations toward his wife as toward his parishioners. Like him, she had been a rebel against the lifelessness of Puritanism; she had married him believing that he, too, wanted a creative life of richness and variety, only to discover that his was the romanticism of a dead past. Taking to drink, one night in Memphis, in a room where she had gone with a stranger, she had committed suicide.

Outraged by the scandal, Hightower's parishioners had locked him out of the church and demanded that he leave town. This he refused to do, even though he was beaten by the Ku Klux Klan; all the meaning of his life was here. In this allegorical novel built around symbolic figures, only the aging Hightower experiences development as he moves from one height to another. From Byron Burch, who alone befriends him, he learns to abandon false romanticism and to ascend toward true love.

When Byron, the workman who has looked after Lena Grove, asks Hightower for help in caring for the ostracized woman during the last days of her pregnancy, he at first refuses with the puritanical phrases of his seminary theology. But in this Christmas story, Byron in the role of Joseph finally persuades the old man to deliver the baby.

Byron has placed Lena in Christmas's abandoned shack because none of the respectable people will take her in, and no one will help in her delivery. When Hightower successfully delivers the baby, he is transformed by his participation in this miracle of the birth of life and, for the first time, he becomes "gentle, beaming, and triumphant." He is redeemed; he has learned to accept the world with love. He has achieved a humility which will help him make those sacrifices that will define him at last as a true minister to the world.

The test of his redemption comes immediately, when Joe Christmas, awaiting trial, learns that Byron Burch and Hightower are planning to help him. Just as in his youth he could not accept the love of Mrs. McEachern because it would violate the code of the separation of white and black, goodness and sin, so now he must defend white supremacy by rejecting this love. He will escape from jail and force the community to lynch him. When he runs, he is pursued by himself, by a young man with the name of Percy Grimm.

The racial crisis expressed in the person of Joe Christmas points to the deeper sickness of Southern society—its inability to accept imperfection. Joe Christmas is a hideous figure of alienation because he believes that he should be perfect and this birthright has been destroyed by the Negro blood within him. In this attitude, he emerges as the representative of the entire white South. The Negro blood within is imaginary as is its taint of imperfection. For Faulkner, white men and black men are brothers. But white Southerners have imagined that black men are different because they have needed to project their guilt upon this scapegoat. In hating the Negro, however, they have hated their own inadequacy, have hated themselves. In lynching the Negro, therefore, they are lynching themselves, just as when Percy Grimm kills Christmas, he will be killing himself. This is the final turn of the circle of self-devouring death.

Percy Grimm is a young man who came to maturity still a confused adolescent. When he joined the National Guard suddenly he could "see his life opening before him, uncomplex and inescapable as a barren corridor, completely freed now of ever having to think or decide, the burden which he now assumed and carried as bright and weightless and martial as his insignatory brass; a sublime and implicit faith in physical courage and blind obedience, and a belief that the white race is superior to any and all other races." In the brilliance of Faulkner's vision Grimm becomes Christmas and Christmas becomes Grimm as they pursue one another.

The flight ends in Hightower's house, with Percy Grimm shooting Christmas and castrating him.

It is a sterile crucifixion because Christmas is filled with hate, not love. As the blood rushes out of his white body, it turns black, as a sign of living death of this society that searches for self-punishment rather than forgiveness. There will be no resurrection and redemption; here, there is no forgiveness of sin.

For Hightower, however, there is light in August, intellectual as well as spiritual. He is no longer bound to the wheel of Southern history. Born again and with the strength to live in the future because he has identified himself with Lena's son, he can reject the impotent romanticism of his grandfather's generation. Now freed from his lifelong attempt to live in a past which never existed, freed from values that have no validity, he is able to understand the people whom he has ignored and refused to minister to; he can find the source of their tragedy in the theology of Puritanism which preached perfection and the punishment of sin. Listening to the church music, "stern and implacable, deliberate and without passion . . . he seems to hear within it the apotheosis  of his own history, his own land. . . . Pleasure, ecstasy, they cannot seem to bear . . . their escape from it is in violence, in drinking and fighting and praying. . . . And so why should not their religion drive them to crucifixion of themselves and one another?" Looking at the church steeples, "He seems to see them, endless, without order, empty, symbolical, bleak, sky-pointed not with ecstasy or passion but in adjuration, threat, and doom. He seems to see the churches of the world like a rampart . . . against that peace in which to sin and be forgiven which is the life of man."

Thus, within the space of a decade, Faulkner discarded his view that the self-reliant, innocent individual represented an absolute good which faced martyrdom at the hands of a corrupt and complex society. By 1931, he was arguing that an individual who defined himself as innocent and self-reliant was a tragic and pathological figure of alienation. This monstrous individual was alienated from the true meaning of life, not from society; a twisted psychopath like Joe Christmas was produced by a society which inculcated the values of personal perfection. It is the genius of Faulkner's art that he is able to make Joe Christmas and Southern society synonymous with one another.

# 2

Robert Penn Warren was the youngest member of the twelve Southerners who contributed to *I'll Take My Stand*. This book of essays, published in 1931, was a call to Yankee intellectuals to find hope in the tradition of Southern agrarianism. The Southern intellectuals argued that Northerners were confused in the 1920's because they had abandoned the true Jeffersonian message that man was to live in harmony with nature, to follow the false promise of progress through industrialism. Now that this faith in progress had collapsed the Lost Generation was invited to return to the timeless verities and perfect harmony of Jeffersonian agrarianism.

At that time Warren was still an adherent to the faith in American uniqueness that promised peace and simplicity to all men, but he had translated national uniqueness into Southern exceptionalism—only in the South did men still escape the terror of history.

His first novel, *Night Rider*, published in 1939, showed how far Warren had broken away from this faith. The book's setting is the tobacco wars which racked Kentucky and Tennessee in the first decade of the twentieth century. In describing the conflict between the small farmers and the large companies which bought their crop, Warren exploded the myth that his region enjoyed harmony because it was close to nature. The central figure of the novel is Percy Munn, a lawyer who becomes a leader of the clandestine farmers' organization—a night rider. Munn is an ordinary man who wants to live his life in peace and therefore avoids commitment. His public life is shaped by circumstances as he follows a line of least resistance to the pressures of the community. Forced by his clients to become a leader of the night riders, ultimately he has to kill a man he would not otherwise have harmed. Warren would seem to be asking if there were any Americans, North or South, East or West, who did not try to save their souls by refusing moral commitment to anything outside of themselves.

His next novel, *At Heaven's Gate,* continues the destruction of his youthful intellectual position. The setting is Vanderbilt University, the city Nashville, the state, Tennessee, and again he is attacking the myth of Southern exceptionalism. The key to the frustrated life Warren depicts is alienation. And the cause of the alienation is a philosophy of self-sufficiency.

The heroine, Sue Murdock, cannot be self-sufficient; she needs the love of a man who is ready to commit himself. Her father, a businessman and political power, is too committed to his career to give her love; his young employee, Jeff Calhoun, too committed to being an observer of the world to accept responsibility for her. The young university intellectual to whom she then turns is a homosexual who is interested only in using Sue to increase his status in the social group. Her last hope is a labor leader who takes her as his mistress to strike out at her father, his economic and political enemy. Sue Murdock can find only death in a society in which all men are committed to a self-fulfillment which selfishly cuts them off from love and moral responsibility.

By World War II, Warren saw clearly that the South was part of national culture and shared with the nation the curse of alienation. But what was the cause of this alienation? Why did Americans believe that self-fulfillment demanded withdrawal from moral responsibility to the community? In *All the King's Men* (1946) he explores the situation in detail.

Warren's instructors at Vanderbilt had taught him that the Lost Generation was lost because it had abandoned Jeffersonianism. Warren now argued that it was lost because it believed in the kind of innocence symbolized by the Jeffersonian dream of arcadia. Jack Burden, the narrator of *All the King's Men,* is a Southerner whose faith in natural perfection died during World War I. Even more than Percy Munn, he is an observer of life, a helpless pawn of the impersonal forces of history, who shuns making decisions which would connect him to other people and rob him of his freedom and his innocence. At the conclusion of the novel, however, he finally accepts the truth that no man is a neutral observer, and that in refusing moral responsibility, he has helped to kill Judge Irwin and Adam Stanton and Willie Stark. The innocent bystander is discovered to be a moral monster. At the story's end he surrenders his burden of innocence and takes up his burden of guilt. He has ceased to define himself as an observer of history and has realized that he is a participant who must assume moral responsibility for his acts.

Jack's father was a successful attorney whose family had given its name to the locality; his mother, a poor girl from Arkansas. When the boy was still small, his father had left home to become a penniless, evangelical preacher to the destitute in the city.

Jack had turned to a neighbor, Judge Irwin, for the personal guidance which he couldn't find at home. And he had found companionship with Adam and Anne Stanton, the children of Governor Stanton, another neighbor. Jack was twenty-one, and Anne seventeen when they fell in love. Finding themselves alone at the end of the summer, Anne was ready to yield to Jack's desire to possess her. But at the final moment, he hesitated, haunted by the image of Anne, the symbol of innocence, floating in the sea. Unconsciously, he was inhibited by the failure of his parent's marriage. Marriage meant the end of perfection, the loss of innocence, the coming of disharmony. Maturity meant an end to childhood romance. Jack thus refused to accept the responsibility of manhood.

When he flunks out in law school and becomes a graduate student in history, his unconscious motivation is clear. He hopes to find in the past the perfection that does not exist in the present, just as he prefers to live with the image of a virginal Anne rather than with the reality of a worldly wife. He describes himself as a philosophical idealist: "I had got hold of the principle out of a book when I was in college, and I had hung on to it for grim death. I owed my success in life to that principle. It had put me where I was. What you don't know don't hurt you, for it ain't real. They called that Idealism in my book I had when I was in college, and after I got hold of that principle I became an Idealist. I was a brass-bound Idealist in those days. If you are an Idealist it does not matter what you do or what goes on around you because it isn't real anyway."

Research for his history dissertation confirms Jack's fears that earthly love leads to earthly hell. "The world is like an enormous spider web and if you touch it, however lightly, at any point, the vibration ripples to the remotest perimeter and the drowsy spider feels the tingle and is drowsy no more but springs out to fling the gossamer coils about you who have touched the web and then inject the black, numbing poison under your hide. It does not matter whether or not you meant to brush the web of things. Your happy foot or your gay wing may have brushed it ever so lightly, but what happens always happens and there is the spider, bearded black, and with his great faceted eyes glittering like mirrors in the sun, or like God's eye, and the fangs dripping." But if the past is as evil as the present, if one cannot impose one's philosophy of idealism upon it, then it does not offer a haven from the terror of the world. Jack Burden, on the verge of achieving his Ph.D., walks away from his unfinished dissertation, and becomes a reporter.

A reporter is an observer who gathers facts but is not responsible for the patterns in which the facts are placed. It was the perfect job for a "brass-bound Idealist"; he was ready to become Willie Stark's man, for Willie too was an idealist of sorts.

Willie Stark, the farm boy from northern Louisiana, had early lost his political innocence, if not his political idealism. Now he will use any means, no matter how foul, to gain the power to do good. Having clawed his way to the top of the ladder and become governor, he accepts the inevitability of evil in this world and uses it to achieve his legislative program. "Man is conceived in sin and born in corruption," he says, "and he passeth from the stink of the didie to the stench of the shroud. There is always something." He finds room in his administration even for men like Tiny Duffy, who has tried to manipulate him in the early stages of his career and whom he will now manipulate in turn.

Jack Burden becomes Willie Stark's henchman, the keeper of his "son-of-a-bitch book." It is his job to find something—"there is always something"—in the past of Willie's friends and enemies against the day when such information may come in handy for the purposes of friendly persuasion. Jack, of course, retains his innocence. He merely uncovers the facts; it is Willie's responsibility how he makes use of them. He will accept no responsibility for political decision, for this would destroy his sense of autonomy and involve him in the web of the spider.

In his own way, Willie shares Jack's philosophy. He too believes that any action will call forth the evil spider. He accepts the inevitability of the spider's bite, but not responsibility for the spider itself. A man who does good for the people can abandon his wife, take on a string of mistresses, corrupt his son, and still continue to believe he is invulnerable. Willie's actions, like Jack's inactions, have no meaningful relationship to other members of the community. He too has no moral responsibility to the individuals who are part of his life. Willie Stark—autonomous power—is the hero of Jack Burden—autonomous innocence.

When his attorney general, Hugh Miller, resigns because Willie refuses to prosecute a member of his administration who is guilty of a felony, Willie lectures him on the nature of the law: "It's like a single-bed blanket on a double-bed and three folks in the bed and a cold night. There ain't ever enough blanket to cover the case, no matter how much pulling and hauling, and somebody is always going to nigh catch pneumonia. . . . The law is always too short and too tight for growing humankind. The best you can do is do something and then make up some law to fit it and by that time that law gets on the books you would have done something different."

"You got to use what you've got," says Willie. "You got to use fellows like . . . Tiny Duffy, and that scum down in the legislature."

Willie decides to build a great hospital for the people; there will be no compromise, no corruption connected with it. To insure this, he asks Jack to persuade his childhood friend, Adam Stanton, who has become a great surgeon, to accept the post of director of the hospital.

Adam Stanton, no less than Jack Burden and Willie Stark, pretends to invulnerability. He is the pure scientist who, in pursuit of what he deems a worthy end, can close his eyes to the dubious means. Whatever qualms he may have had about serving the currupt Stark are brushed aside when he learns that his idealized father, the former Governor Stanton, was not above reproach.

Jack Burden is the source of this information. One of Willie's few remaining major political opponents is Judge Irwin; some scandal must exist in the judge's past that would come in handy now. Jack, who feels a deep affection for this old man who had been the father figure of his past, accepts the assignment of digging into the judge's history, reassuring himself that he will find nothing. But he learns that the judge, when he was Governor Stanton's attorney general, was once desperately in need of money to save his estate from foreclosure, and had somehow acquired the funds. He had used his power as attorney general to rule that a private company did not have to pay the state a large sum of money. The judge's reward was the payment of his mortgage and a well-paid position with the company. And Governor Stanton, pressed to investigate, had refused. This was the history of their father that Jack now imparted to Adam Stanton and his sister Anne. It helped bring Adam into Willie Stark's circle. It also helped to make Anne, the girl who might have been his, Willie's mistress.

Jack Burden, who had always tried to avoid action because action can cause evil, cannot hide from the feeling that his own inaction has just as surely called forth the spider. Was there no escape from responsibility? No longer the "brass-bound Idealist," he tries to rationalize his situation. Actions are real, he decides, but they are morally meaningless. They are merely expressions of "the Great Twitch." Man makes no decisions through free will; all his decisions are determined by his body chemistry. He was not really responsible for what Anne had become. According to the law of the "Great Twitch . . . you are never guilty of a crime you did not commit."

Fortified by his new philosophy, Jack continues to serve Willie Stark, who is planning to move up to the United States Senate. To get there, Willie must neutralize his old political opponent MacMurfee and to do this he must get Judge Irwin to withdraw his support of MacMurfee by threatening to expose the old scandal that Jack Burden has dug up. The judge kills himself, and Jack learns that the man who had acted as his father was in fact his father.

Now at last Jack Burden begins to see that good and evil exist side by side. Judge Irwin had sinned and yet he had been a good man. His mother, too, had sinned, and yet she had loved the man who fathered her son. For the first time, Jack's mind is opened to the possibility that life is a moral drama in which every action or inaction has moral significance. Even so, he is not yet ready to surrender his illusion of innocence and accept the burden of guilt. The last act of the drama has still to be played out.

It opens with an anonymous phone call to Adam Stanton from Tiny Duffy, the man Willie Stark has always treated as something inhuman and who now proves his humanity by an act of hatred; Adam learns of his sister's relationship to Willie. It ends with Adam's murder of Willie and his own death at the hand of Willie's bodyguard, Sugarboy.

Surely Jack's inaction has not been responsible for the death of Adam and Willie, any more than for Anne's involvement or Judge Irwin's suicide. Or has it? Still unwilling to face himself, he dreams of making Duffy the scapegoat for his own guilt. He has only to advise Sugar-boy of Duffy's treacherous phone call to effect the deed. As he sits alone in the public library dreaming of revenge, he sees Duffy's face winking at him; if he kills Duffy he will be Duffy himself. He and Duffy are brothers in crime; they have been brothers in all the crimes of the Stark administration.

Jack, who must be isolated from humanity as long as he does not accept his own guilt, realizes that where there is no past there is no future. Now that he can accept the guilt for the past, he is freed to live in the future.

He remembers Willie's dying words, "It might have been all different, Jack." The greatness of Willie Stark and of Adam Stanton lay in their ability to act; it was the will to act that had given them dignity. But both men were cursed by the same philosophy of personal invulnerability. This was why "each had killed the other. Each had been the doom of the other. As a student of history, Jack Burden could see that Adam Stanton, whom he came to call the man of idea, and Willie Stark, whom he came to call the man of fact, were doomed to destroy each other, just as each was doomed to try to use the other and to yearn toward and try to become the other, because each was incomplete with the terrible division of their age. But . . . though doomed they had nothing to do with any doom under the godhead of the Great Twitch. They were doomed, but they lived in the agony of will."

Jack Burden had tried to live as an observer of the world of idea and the world of fact; he had tried to avoid the agony of will. Like his father in fact, he had dreamed of a world of perfect peace and harmony, and like his father in name he had tried to retreat from the world as it existed. The latter had given his son a burden of innocence which prevented his accepting responsibility toward the woman he loved. But Judge Irwin, in giving his son the knowledge of guilt, gave him the strength to accept his involvement in the world of idea and fact, the will to create the future out of his acceptance of the past. Reborn at forty, Jack Burden is the first Warren hero to accept the responsibility of a woman's love. It is late, but not too late, to marry Anne Stanton and to step "out of history into history and the awful responsibility of Time."

For Warren, as for Faulkner, the concern for alienation was intensely personal. Each had come to define himself as an alienated man and had searched for the ideological cause of his alienation. Each had found it in the philosophy of perfection, the concept of earthly saintliness, which had been the dominant outlook of the Southern community in which they had reached maturity. They had come to relate this regional belief in a heavenly city on earth to the larger national culture and beyond that to western civilization itself. In the 1930's, each had discovered for himself the great insights of Nathaniel Hawthorne.

The tragedy of Jack Burden might be viewed as that prophesied by Hawthorne when he warned that until Dimmesdale accepted responsibility for his daughter, a responsibility which demanded the father's revelation of his own relationship to the Eternal Adam, Pearl must remain alienated from the community; she could never become fully human. She needed "a grief that should deeply touch her, and thus humanize and make her capable of sympathy," and this grief would spring from the discovery of her link to the fallible nature of humanity.

For Warren, Jack Burden was impotent within the prison of his belief in the perfection of invulnerability. As long as he viewed himself as the son of a sinless father, he remained alienated from community. It was only when Jack discovered he was linked to the Eternal Adam that he experienced a grief which could deeply touch him and thus humanize and make him capable of sympathy.

At the conclusion of World War II, Robert Penn Warren had renewed the warning of Hawthorne—Americans were fated to sterile alienation unless they acknowledged the centrality of grief to their experience, unless they acknowledged the need for both law and love.

## 3

The American intellectual community in the years after 1945 did not take up Warren's burden of history, with its awful responsibility of constantly making and remaking the timeful synthesis of idea and fact which is both man's necessary fate and his freedom. Instead, the majority of American intellectuals found a formula which made it possible for them to achieve the appearance of becoming historical realists without abandoning the tradition of the timeless American Garden.

After World War II, Americans could no longer indulge in the kind of nostalgia for the lost frontier of nature which had informed the writings of Hemingway. Nor could they rekindle the naive faith of a progressive historian like Beard, who had seen industrialism as a new frontier force that would inevitably destroy the social structure of institutions and traditions and restore the American Adam to an earthly paradise. But if Eden could be found neither in the past nor in the future, why might it not be discovered in the present?

To argue the perfection of the status quo demanded a major redefinition of both the American Eden and the American Adam. It was necessary to justify the growth of the urban-industrial complexity which had so disturbed the people of the United States in the closing decades of the nineteenth century and to demonstrate that the ever-increasing multiplicity of institutions and traditions did not herald the return of the human condition of the Old World. Again it is historians who most clearly outline the promise of that organic natural unity of value and fact which supposedly underlies our national uniqueness. And of these it is Professor Daniel Boorstin of the University of Chicago who most seriously aspires to replace Beard and Bancroft as the theoretician of American perfection.

When Boorstin insists, "that the whole American experience has been utopian," * his strategy begins with the affirmation that European traditions and institutions did cross the Atlantic. European man brought European traditions and institutions across the ocean and used them to build the foundations of a new society. In Europe, according to Boorstin, man inherited institutions and traditions within the context of an established historical society and was, therefore, the prisoner of his civilization. But when the European crossed the Atlantic, he used these institutions and traditions as the tools to adjust to nature and to build a new society. The European became that new man, the American, because in the New World the individual controlled his institutions and traditions in a society designed to bring and keep men in harmony with nature. Social complexity in America was organically related to nature, and its only purpose was to express individual freedom.

This meant that "The most fertile novelty of the New World [was] its new concept of knowledge. . . . The time

---

*Daniel Boorstin, *The Genius of American Politics* (Chicago, 1953).

had come for the over-cultivated man of Europe to re-discover the earth on which he walked." Americans gave up the tradition of abstract learning for practical education; they did not want philosophers but good citizens. Philosophy and theology were unnecessary when men had achieved the materialist utopia. "Was not the New World a living denial of the old sharp distinction between the world as it was and the world as it might be or ought to be?"

If it is true that "the genius of American democracy comes not from any special virtue of the American people but from the unprecedented opportunities of this continent and from a peculiar and unrepeatable combination of human circumstance," then the only freedom of God's chosen people must be the conservation of God's gift. "Our history has fitted us . . . to understand the meaning of conservatism. . . . The unspoiled grandeur of America helped men believe that here the Giver of values spoke to man more directly—in the language of experience rather than in that of books and monuments."

This is why, Boorstin concludes, we must firmly isolate ourselves from the continental Europeans whose historical traditions and institutions do not embody natural law and who must turn to abstract political theory in a vain attempt to imitate God's creation in America. Europeans must also turn to abstract theology as still another ideological attempt to escape the disharmony of history. But, he warns, Americans should not let their imaginations wander along the lines of European political theory or theology. Let us always remember that God has given us a good society and we find our political and spiritual values within its structure. This is why American "religions are instrumental. They commend themselves to us for the services they perform more than the truths which they affirm."

For Daniel Boorstin, historian of American uniqueness in the 1950's, the metaphysics of George Bancroft and Charles Beard had become irrelevant. His triumphant message was that from 1600 to the present European institutions and traditions had always been the foundation of social reality in America. Bancroft's Garden of absolute simplicity had never existed and Beard's promise could never be fulfilled. But since Americans used these Old World institutions and traditions pragmatically, their relation to social complexity was that of freedom, while Europeans, approaching culture through ideology, were slaves to society. Boorstin's ultimate promise then was that in the New World everything that is is right. Freedom was the recognition of necessity. It would follow, therefore, within the logic of Boorstin's metaphysics, as in Bancroft's or Beard's, that the European art form, the novel, could not flourish in the United States. Here there could be neither the tragedy nor comedy of manners because every institution or tradition was pragmatically useful to the expression of individual personality. Nor could there be the tragedy or comedy of individual pretension to personal transcendence because the American, by definition, was a pragmatic realist who refused the temptation of the romantic dream. The American was content to find his values within the given.

As Beard's historical metaphysics had found their most popular expression in the novels of Winston Churchill, so Boorstin's found theirs in the novel of James Gould Cozzens, *By Love Possessed*, which was published in 1957 and sold one hundred and seventy thousand copies within seven weeks.

Arthur Winner, middle-aged lawyer and member of the aristocracy of a small eastern town, is chosen by Cozzens to carry the burden of initiating Americans into the reality of existence, to demonstrate the necessity of conducting oneself as a Man of Reason and accepting the status quo.

At fifty-four Arthur Winner, twice married and the father of one rebellious son and another who committed suicide, felt that he was providing sensible leadership to his

community. His profession, the law, provided human stability: it was law and justice, not theology and love, which
made life worth living. Man was not free to transcend the
institutions and traditions of society. But he was free to use
those institutions and traditions to fulfill his earthly needs
and bring provisional order out of chaos. It was this sense
of the solidity of the arch of social structure, made whole
by the keystone of the law, that gave Arthur the assurance
that the American way was not lost in the second half of
the twentieth century. Into the United States had come
alien people—Jews, Catholics, and Negroes. If the American
way meant perfect freedom of the individual from all cultural interference, then this alien invasion was catastrophic.
But if true Americanism was the achievement of justice
through the pragmatic manipulation of institutions and
traditions, then these strangers could be taught to become
responsible citizens who recognized the need to accept the
status quo.

Arthur Winner would teach his fellow Anglo-Saxon
Protestant aristocrats that they could accept these new
Americans without endangering their values of social conservatism. He introduces the New York City lawyer, Woolf,
to his friends to show them that Woolf was eager to overcome his Jewish shortcomings and learn the qualities of
restraint which characterized the establishment. He persuades his fellow lawyers to accept Jerry Brophy, the son of
the Irish saloon-keeper from across the tracks, who now
aspires to become a judge, because Brophy has rejected the
values of the lower class and accepted those of the establishment. He accepts the "good" Negro who treats white
people with courteous respect. In short Arthur Winner views
his America with a sense of security, not to say self-satisfac-
tion.

As a Man of Reason, "uncluttered by the irrelevant,
uncolored by the emotional thinker's futile wishing and

excesses of false feeling," he despises theology. He agrees with his partner, Julius Penrose, that "theology could be said to be a homage nonsense tries to pay to sense." But he is of course, a churchgoer. Indeed, he is a pillar of the Episcopal church, a vestryman who explains his philosophy of church-going expediency in these words: "The man who is reasonable takes with civil accommodation reasonable account of his fellows, of the feelings and beliefs that comfort or calm the great majority of minds neither detached, dispassionate, nor tempered well. . . . Professed skepticism was a vulgar sin against taste. . . . The Man of Reason made himself, with decent devoutness, a regular communicant."

In the same way, Arthur Winner feels the need to educate the new Episcopalian rector, Dr. Trowbridge, to the reality of his responsibility. Fresh from seminary, and filled with the scholarly and naive belief that it was his function to save souls through the preaching of the gospel, Dr. Trowbridge has to be taught that his role is a practical one: to keep his congregation financially sound, to smooth hurt feelings, and to perform the traditional routines which provide structure for his group. He must learn that his is primarily a worldly, not otherworldly, leadership.

But beneath the surface of his stoic calm and reasonableness, Arthur Winner is not unacquainted with the feeling of guilt. Some years ago, after his first wife had died, he had had a brief, violent affair with Marjorie, the wife of his partner, Julius Penrose. He had never been able to justify or explain his action to himself, but the sense of guilt, the knowledge that he had betrayed his friend, remained.

Now a new load of guilt is added to him. He is incapable of true charity toward another. When Helen Detweiler, the secretary of his law firm, for whom he feels a sympathetic and protective regard, comes to him for help for her younger brother, who has run afoul of the law, he fails her and she commits suicide. She had asked for the bread of understanding, and he had given her the stone of reason.

And then, while going over some of her papers, he discovers that Noah Tuttle, the ancient senior member of the firm and the father of Arthur's first wife, has embezzled large sums of money from the Episcopal church's trust fund. Suddenly the real world of the Man of Reason seems unbearable. Can he go on with the guilt of Marjorie and of Helen on his conscience, with his knowledge of the dereliction of his partner and father-in-law?

It is Julius Penrose, the absolute Man of Reason, who counsels him in his time of trial, offering expediency in the name of wisdom.

Arthur need feel no guilt for Helen's suicide, Julius maintains; she was predestined for self-destruction. "On the world she never made, she imposed with all her strength a pattern of the world she wanted." It was pity, not guilt, that one should feel toward a person who is "mad, possessed by love." Nothing would have prevented her ultimate rejection of a world which refused to conform to her standards.

Furthermore, Julius continues, he had always known of Arthur's brief interlude with Marjorie and appreciated the fact that he had tried to keep the knowledge of this unpleasant situation from him. Like Helen, Marjorie too was "mad, possessed by love." She too was to be pitied. But no man could feel guilty about her actions. The Man of complete Reason will understand that a man invited to bed by an attractive woman will assent. "I venture to assert that when this gadfly's sting is fairly driven in, when the indefeasible urge of the flesh presses them, few men of normal potency prove able to refrain their foot from that path." Given Marjorie's nymphomaniac irresponsibility, what Arthur had done was biological determinism, clearly beyond

his control. The Man of Reason recognized that he could
not escape the laws of nature. Hence there was no guilt.

Finally, Julius turns to the case of Noah Tuttle. From
the moment he had joined the firm more than a decade
earlier, he had discovered Noah's financial problem. The
old man had taken funds from the trusts he controlled, such
as those of the Episcopal church, to cover the losses of
members of the community. Speculating on the stock
market, he was gradually replacing the depleted funds.
Why, Julius asked, should he have revealed his discovery?
What purpose would it serve to ruin the career of this
honorable old man? Or the trusts which were slowly being
rebuilt? Why should he ruin the life of Arthur Winner and
his family? Or his own career, for that matter? What choice
did they have but to carry on or face utter ruin? "Shun
immediate evils is the wise, or at least the smart man's
maxim," Julius declares. "As a wise old man once said to
me: Boy, never try to piss up the wind. Principle must
sometimes be shelved."

Arthur Winner is dedicated to the law, and despite
Julius's philosophy of expediency, his conscience tells him
he should reveal the violation of his clients' trusts by Noah.
But then the law in its wisdom said: "No man shall be judge
of his own cause . . . the law, nothing but reason, took
judicial notice of man's nature, of how far his conscience
could guide him against his interest. For the sake of others,
for his own sake, the law would not let him be led into
temptation." Julius was right, and conscience was wrong.
Rejecting the abstract, the unreal standards of conscience,
Arthur Winner passes the final test and becomes, like Julius,
the complete Man of Reason.

# VI

---

# THE PRESENT

---

*Norman Mailer*
*James Baldwin*
*Saul Bellow*

**1**

When *By Love Possessed* was universally hailed as the great American novel, it became clear that if the intellectual community in the United States, at the beginning of the second half of the twentieth century, could no longer use the myth of the American Adam in a creative fashion, neither would it abandon the traditional definition of the national community. Dedicated to a sterile conservation of a bankrupt ideal, Americans were evidently prepared to remain loyal to an aging, impotent, and misanthropic Adam in a Garden that was rapidly becoming a barren desert.

This national consensus, doggedly committed to an ideal that no longer inspires hope, provides the key to our understanding the novels of protest in the nineteen fifties and sixties, which have shattered the rational world of Arthur Winner. When one turns to the works of Norman Mailer and James Baldwin, one has apparently left the civilized world of middle-class consensus to explore a dark and untamed foreign continent. But only apparently, because Mailer and Baldwin remain loyal to the heart of the national faith that the United States is to be the Garden of the world and its inhabitants reborn Adams. Their writings are filled with the grotesque, the perverse, the criminal, even the insane, as these authors grope for new ways to restore the American Garden to beauty and the American Adam to vigor.

Like James Gould Cozzens, they agree that it is not possible to restore the agrarian simplicity of George Bancroft. More reluctantly, they also agree that industrialism will not automatically bring another type of organic and primitive harmony. But if they feel that the historical analysis of Bancroft and Beard is no longer tenable, they do not share the new conservatism of Boorstin which proclaims the current establishment is itself only a complex expression of organic harmony. For the younger novelists the present establishment of complex institutions, of massive corporations and bureaucracy and armed forces, is a gigantic parasitical growth which increasingly contaminates the American Garden and suffocates the native Adam; the very citadel of the American dream is being undermined by the growth of this social monster. If their efforts to reverse this process seem at times to be desperate and even hysterical, it is because they see no plausible way to reverse the historical process from frontier simplicity to civilized complexity. And since they refuse to rationalize this complexity away, and reject the formulas of Boorstin and Cozzens, they must of necessity search for the implausible way, the irrational way, to destroy history and restore the Garden. Such is the terrifying burden of innocence which is expressed in the tormented novels of Norman Mailer and James Baldwin.

Mailer catapulted into national prominence with his first novel, *The Naked and the Dead,* published in 1948. Mailer's platoon represented a cross section of America, men from the South and North, East and West, Catholic, Jew, and Protestant, Anglo-Saxon, Latin, and Slav. Each man was found spiritually and morally wanting, a sick member of a sick society, and each sought a scapegoat who could be held responsible. The animal viciousness of the platoon members was qualified by the Protestant fundamentalist from rural America, Ridge, and the fundamentalist Jew from the city, Goldstein. Only these two were capable of pity and charity. But in turning the other cheek, they put themselves completely at the mercy of the power structure of the platoon, the company, the regiment, the army, the American establishment. If Mailer despised the selfishness and fear of the others, he also despaired of the generosity and love of these impotent saints. Indeed, rage at his own impotence is the central theme of this novel as it is the central theme of each of Mailer's subsequent books.

The character who most clearly speaks for the author is Lieutenant Hearn. Hearn is the son of a self-made, Midwestern businessman, a graduate of Harvard who has rejected the sterile philosophy of material success of his father, but has found no new set of values which seem worthy of his commitment. At college, he had flirted with Marxism but was not able to accept that faith, any more than later he was capable of making meaningful relationships with others. Convinced of the worthlessness of American society, Hearn had become a cynical observer who gave meaning to his life through his pride that he was more free from ridiculous social concerns than any of his friends.

Now he had become part of the army but nothing had changed. He was merely trapped within another form of the establishment. Here, however, he was in closer proximity to the men of authority who provided leadership for the imprisoning institutions of society. "He despised the six field officers at the adjacent table because no matter how much they might hate kikes, niggers, Russians, limeys, micks, they loved one another . . . got drunk together without worrying about dropping their guard. . . . By their very existence they had warped the finest minds, the most brilliant talents of Hearn's generation into something sick. . . . You always ended by catering to them, or burrowing fearfully into the little rathole still allowed."

Assigned directly as an aid to General Cummings, Hearn finds himself confronted by a strong, intelligent man who challenges his pose as a cynical observer of the social structure. You are like me, the General tells him, because you want to assert your individuality, you want to express your will freely, and you believe that to be free you must not compromise with the establishment. But "You're a fool if you don't realize this is going to be the reactionary's century, perhaps their thousand year reign." The only way to escape being a slave of institutions is to control them, the general says. Your lack of commitment, your cynicism does not save you from having to obey the establishment. The only meaningful freedom is power over institutions.

If Lieutenant Hearn is unable to refute this argument, Mailer is determined to demonstrate that neither can freedom be gained in attempting to bend institutions to the individual's will. Although the general expends all of his intelligence to forge a plan that will flank the Japanese lines, and wills the fulfillment of his strategy through the flow of his orders down the chain of command, the Japanese line is broken by the blundering of Major Dalleson. Inevitably, the orders of the General are lost in the complexity and confusion of the institutional structure and the fallibility of the men who try to run it.

When Hearn, the liberal, attempts to lead the institutional unit, the platoon, over which the General has given him command, he is killed by Sergeant Croft, who refuses to surrender his control. But Croft, too, fails to find freedom through institutional control. His attempts to force the men over an almost impossible mountain through sheer will power comes to nothing when they are attacked by hornets and take flight.

If the liberal, through his inaction, must remain the prisoner of the malignant establishment, and if the man of strength finds only frustration or death by attempting to control the establishment, what hope could Mailer provide that the American Adam was ultimately to triumph over social complexity and restore the American garden? His second novel, *Barbary Shore,* his weakest artistic effort, attempts to explore this dilemma to its last possible extreme. If there was some doubt that Lieutenant Hearn spoke for the author, there is none that the nameless hero of this book speaks for Norman Mailer.

Mikey Lovett, Mailer's orphan hero, is the traditional American Adam who, like Leatherstocking, takes his start outside of time, even though his space is a Brooklyn slum. Mikey Lovett cannot act because he has no goals, no values, no commitments. Why is he trapped in the sterility of a Brooklyn tenement? For Mailer, Mikey Lovett's situation is the American condition. History as liberal progress, as Marxist progress, has failed; as defined by the pre-World War II generation, it has no meaning. Mikey, like his creator, Norman Mailer, seaches for meaning in the midst of total confusion.

In the tenement live two men, the timid, intellectual, middle-aged clerk, McLeod, and the young, neat, brash clerk, Hollingsworth—McLeod, the disillusioned Communist who is too old to find a new faith to give meaning to his life; and Hollingsworth, an agent of the American capitalist bureaucratic establishment. Hollingsworth has stepped into the vacuum left by the collapse of McLeod's faith. Soon he will kill McLeod and take away his wife and child. At the end of the novel, Mikey Lovett is still a pilgrim searching for meaning. All he has in his loneliness is McLeod's last will and testament, which prophecies the destruction of civilization by the two great bureaucracies of the East and West, but which promises the possibility of something new and better which will rise from the ruins.

For McLeod, it was inevitable that the bureaucracy of state capitalism and the bureaucracy of monopoly capitalism would wage war against one another; "From out the unyielding contradictions of labor stolen from men, the march to the endless war forces its pace." The fatal mistake of socialists, McLeod warned, was to assume that progress from complexity to simplicity was inevitable. Socialists, therefore, did not adequately guard against the growth of new forms of social complexity until suddenly they found themselves trapped by modern bureaucracy.

The implications for the education of Mikey Lovett were clear. He must work out a theory of personal activism to control the course of history, and this activism must be an expression of the will of the individual. Mailer's next novel, *The Deer Park*, was to take a tentative step in the direction of creating such a philosophy.

Mailer took his title from Mouffle d'Angerville's *Vie Privée de Louis XV*, which described "the Deer Park, that gorge of innocence and virtue in which were engulfed so many victims who when they returned to society brought with them depravity, debauchery and all the vices they naturally acquired from the infamous officials of such a place." Into the American Deer Park, the Desert D'Or, Hollywood's plushest vacation resort, comes another orphan hero, Sergius O'Shaugnessy. This American Adam, like Mikey Lovett, had no start within "space as spaciousness" as the "realm of total possibility." Instead, he began life within the prison of social institutions, and he must liberate himself from the blandishments of society, which constantly tempt him to accept this environment as normal. Inevitably, of course, he will preserve his innocence.

Sergius O'Shaugnessy has grown up within the institutional structure of a Catholic orphanage, and exchanged this secure home for another, the United States Air Force. He had gone to the Far East to drop liquid fire on Asians. Raised to see the world as a series of abstractions and stereotypes, he had never questioned his way of life. He had no conscience about his giving of death until one day he saw a burn on the arm of his Japanese mess boy. Suddenly, he was able to see beneath the façade of the establishment; he saw the bottomless depths of horror which were disguised by patriotic slogans. No longer could he kill men without feeling. He had a nervous breakdown and was discharged.

Now he has come to the Desert D'Or because "it was better not even to think of this" real world of war. "I did not want to feel too much, and I did not want to think." In his overt flight from reality, in his desire to forget his confrontation with reality within the artificial world of Hollywood, Sergius is the archetypical American, except in one aspect; he has the power of critical observation and analysis which ultimately can liberate him. He sees clearly the pattern of Hollywood society. At the top are the giant producers, the Emperors, like Herman Teppis, a moral monster who mouths the platitudes of patriotism and morality and demands that his writers, directors, and actors make movies according to formulas which titillated the public and which made money. He forces his subjects to prostrate themselves before him politically, intellectually, morally, and sexually.

Then there are directors like Charles Eitel who have lost their artistic vision. Eitel has no meaningful philosophy of life; without a reason for rejecting the pseudopatriotism and materialism of the establishment, he surrenders to the temptation to have authority within the power structure. At the other extreme of this sterile world is Marion O'Faye, the son of Dorothea O'Faye, who has become rich as the mistress of a series of wealthy men. Marion openly makes his living as a pimp. As he sees it, Americans pretend to moral respectability but, committed to economic exploitation, to the coming of war, to propaganda in the forms of entertainment which diverts attention from reality, every American must become a pimp or a whore, even as Eitel is in relation to Teppis.

Marion cannot visualize any way to escape this vast spiderweb of corruption except through death. As he looks east toward the atomic testing grounds in Nevada, he prays: "Let this explosion come, and then another, and all the others, until the Sun God burned the earth. Let it come, like a man praying for rain, let it come and clear the rot and the stink, let it come for all of us everywhere, just so it comes and the world stands clear in the white dead dawn."

Sergius O'Shaugnessy rejects the nihilism of Marion O'Faye, and the surrender of Charles Eitel. Rejecting, too, the lure of women, gold, and power, he leaves the Desert D'Or and Hollywood to go to New York to become an artist. "Do try, Sergius," counsels Eitel, "try for that other world, the real world, where orphans burn orphans and nothing is more difficult to discover than a simple fact. And with the pride of an artist, you must blow against the walls of every power that exists, the small trumpet of your defiance."

Sergius escapes Eitel's surrender to the establishment and Marion O'Faye's nihilism because he has discovered God. He has found a source of power which lifts him above the impotence of Lieutenant Hearn and Mikey Lovett. In overcoming his sexual impotence, he has found the spiritual significance of sex. Conversing with God at the end of the novel, Sergius asks if "sex is where philosophy begins?" and God replies, "Rather think of sex as time and time as the connection of new circuits."

For the next five years, Norman Mailer attempted to develop a new philosophy of hope built around his faith that sex was the means to transcend the institutions and traditions of society; it would provide the power the individual needed to destroy historical culture. Sex was the basis of a new frontier experience in which the American Adam could once again exist in "space as spaciousness," as "the realm of total possibility"; it was to be the foundation of a restored New World Garden in which the American Adam would live in total innocence according to God's law rather than that of man.

In his essays of the late fifties, Mailer developed his argument that there was a unique American Adam, the American existentialist, who was gathering strength for an ultimate revolution against society. His name is the hipster; his code, to "accept the terms of death, to live with death as immediate danger, to divorce oneself from society, to exist without roots, to set out on the uncharted journey into the rebellious imperatives of the self." The hipster understands that one must be "a frontiersman in the Wild West of American night life, or else a square cell, trapped in the totalitarian tissues of American society."

The Negro, according to Mailer, was the ideal American Adam who lived in the realm of total possibility. Denied a place in society, the Negro was never trapped within the institutions and traditions of history; he had to practice "the art of the primitive," to live "in the enormous present." The hipster is the white man who has taken the primitive, asocial Negro for his model and has accepted the Negro's approach to God through the orgasm; jazz is his sacred music. This is why the hipster, the American existentialist, is unique to the New World. "To be a real existentialist, one must be religious, one must have one's sense of the 'purpose,' " and European existentialists are not religious. Committed to atheism and rationalism, they lack the dynamic link to God which the American hipster has and are therefore impotent in the face of the historical ash heap of traditions and institutions which make Europe a spiritual desert. Here in the New World, however, the American hipster has the inspiration to become a warrior of God, a true believer. The hipster knows then that God's victory over the powers of darkness, which are embodied in society, depends upon the victory of each individual.

It is clear from his essays that midway through the decade between *The Deer Park* and *An American Dream,* Mailer had reached a philosophical and theological crisis. He had begun these crucial ten years preaching that a moral, a religious revolution had begun in America, led by the priestly hipsters who were teaching the people to escape their social sinfulness through the grace given by sex. But at the end of the 1950's, he had come to the demoralizing conclusion that the high priests of sex were incapable of effecting such a revolution. The forces of darkness were not only entrenched in the institutions and traditions of society, they had infiltrated the inner citadel of the human soul as well.

Suddenly, Mailer was no longer concerned with liberating mankind from civilization, but only with the salvation of his own soul. The bleak vision which runs through his essays at the beginning of the 1960's is that of "a modern soul marooned in constipation, emptiness, boredom, and a flat dull terror of death." Mailer is no longer the holy psychopath preaching the power of sex to destroy the establishment. Here he is terrified of the evil within his own heart: "The scatology is within and not without. The urge to eat another does not exist in some cannibal we watch in the jungle, but in the hinge of our own jaws. . . . These morbid states . . . can obtain relief only by coming to life in the psyche." He explains the suicide of his hero, Hemingway, as a result of his failure to face "his dirty ape, id, or antisocial impulse. . . . So long as Hemingway did not test himself, push himself beyond his own dares, flirt with, engage, and finally embrace death . . . so long as he did not propitiate the dwarf, give the dwarf its chance to live and feel emotion . . . Hemingway and the dwarf were doomed to dull and deaden one another in the dungeons of the psyche."

By the middle of the 1960's, Mailer was ready to join

Captain Ahab. He would conquer the white whale he had discovered in himself even if it meant the destruction of all those who shipped on the Pequod. Violence was the means of personal purification. *An American Dream*, published in 1965, is a frantic and hysterical effort of the American Adam to escape from time and to regain the sanctity of George Bancroft's forest where, as an orphan hero, the American can once more begin in "space as spaciousness, as the unbounded, the area of total possibility."

Stephen Rojack, the hero of this novel, has gone to Congress in 1946 with his eye clearly on the Presidency, but he has deliberately thrown away the possibilities of political power by backing Wallace, while his fellow congressman, Jack Kennedy, had kept to the straight and narrow path of rational success. Rojack had learned in the war that there were dark depths of fear and hatred in his soul, and he was coming to believe that worldly success was meaningless unless he could save his soul.

In his quest for self-knowledge, Rojack becomes a professor of psychology only to compromise himself with the demands of the university as institution, and to compromise himself further by marrying Deborah Coughlin Mangaravidi Kelly, daughter of a self-made multimillionaire.

Now in his forties, a worldly success, Rojack is separated from his wife. He feels that he has surrendered his strength, his independence, his personality, in giving his love to Deborah. Psychically bleeding to death, he is tempted to commit suicide, when suddenly it occurs to him that man reaches God not through love but courage, not through dependence but independence. Resolutely he goes home to face Deborah, and when she meets him with tales of her unfaithfulness that are designed to push him still further toward death, he kills her.

He has asserted his ego, he has acted without regard to social consequences. He has learned that the brave are free because men in society are motivated by fear, and the individual who chooses courage becomes a superman able to dominate the craven citizens who are prisoners of their concern for consequences. The superman forces one of the maids to bow to his sexual demands, throws his wife's body out of the window, and leaves the house to engage in a battle of will against the police. Another sexual bout that evening, another session the next morning with the police, who finally accept his story of Deborah's suicide, and Rojack, the courageous, is a free man, free to develop his psychological insight that "God was not love but courage." Now he could "blow up Freud by demonstrating that the root of neurosis is cowardice and not the Oedipus complex."

This he does by returning to the lady of the night before and beating up her Negro lover. But the test of his salvation, the test of his courage, is not yet concluded. He has yet to confront Deborah's father. He goes to the Waldorf, where he learns that Barney Kelly not only controls the Mafia, the Black Muslims, and the CIA, but even the *New York Times*. This peerless manipulator of the institutional power of the establishment dares him to walk the railing of his terrace many stories above Park Avenue to prove that he has become a man of limitless courage. Rojack does, and when Barney tries to push him off he strikes down his opponent and presumably the power he represents.

Rojack now leaves New York for Las Vegas, where he wills his victory over the gaming tables. He has withdrawn his allegiance from the United States, which had failed to fulfill the European dream of a New World frontier. Purged of the dirty ape within by his acts of courage, he has achieved freedom from the jungle of the American establishment. A clean ape once more, he heads toward a new frontier because "There was a jungle somewhere in Guatemala which had a friend, an old friend. I thought to go there. And on to Yucatan."

## 2

In the escape of Rojack from the corrupt society of the United States to the sanctuary of an unspoiled state of nature, Norman Mailer had vicariously fulfilled an American dream. He had tried to re-establish the American Adam, to make the "hero in space," dwelling in "the area of total possibility." But Rojack fulfilled the warning of Cooper that Leatherstocking, existing in space rather than time, was exiled from the area of possibility. In his perfect solitude, Leatherstocking was sterile; no fruitful creativity was allowed him in the wilderness. In achieving the perfect freedom of the American dream, Rojack had attained that isolated state of perfect nothingness predicted by Cooper, Hawthorne, Melville, and James as the end which awaited the American Adam.

The novels of James Baldwin also culminate in the sterility of saintliness rooted in spaciousness rather than time. Baldwin, as a Negro, has attempted to make spiritual capital out of the Mailer thesis that Negroes remain an uncorrupted band of saints within the general corruption of white society. He has added his personal hallelujah to Mailer's praise of the continuing alienation of the Negro from his white neighbors. And he has paralleled Mailer in abandoning hope for national regeneration by an elect group of saints. In his most recent novel, *Another Country,* he too can offer hope only to those solitary saints who have the strength to reject the eternal temptation of the sinners who will always dominate society.

His first novel, *Go Tell It on the Mountain,* is strongly autobiographical, focusing on the coming of age of John Grimes who, like himself, is the son of a New York City evangelical preacher. The Grimes family lives in the

earthly hell of a Harlem tenement which, for Baldwin,
represents the place of the Negro in white America—
nothing but the most abject and degrading poverty. And
this poverty, spiritual as well as physical, is the gift of
the white man to the black.

Rejecting his father, the boy Johnny has also rejected
his father's hatred of white society. He refuses to believe
that their particular congregation of black saints was completely surrounded by sinful whites. What he had to learn
before he could become a leader of his people, was that
Gabriel Grimes, his father—actually his stepfather—was the
prisoner of the white devils, and his theology of damnation
the doctrine of a sick white society.

If Gabriel symbolizes the tragedy of the Negro attempting to live by white doctrines, his wife, mother of
the illegitimate Johnny, represents the tragedy of the Negro
who attempts to live outside of white doctrines. Elizabeth
had come north with the man she loved, who was a rebel
against the sterile Puritanism which the white man had
imposed on the Negro. But while the North had promised
him more, "what it promised it did not give, and what it
gave, at length and grudgingly with one hand, it took back
with the other." Finally compelled to realize that he must
always be the prisoner of white society, he had committed
suicide. Elizabeth had then accepted Gabriel's offer of marriage because he seemed to offer her the protection she
needed for herself and her son against a hostile white
world. But now she was coming to see that Gabriel was
trying to thrust Johnny out of the Negro group because he
could not accept the innate goodness of Negro spontaneity which Johnny represented.

Gabriel was a true stepfather to this child of the Negro
race. He demanded theological innocence when the theological experience of the Negro was suffering. He called
for a theological rejection of the joys of the flesh when

the experience of the Negro was the spiritual redemption found in the spontaneous expression of his instincts.

Always Johnny had fought conversion to his father's faith, appalled by its vicious denial of human instinct, but one day he suddenly found himself seized by a power stronger than himself and thrown speechless to the floor of the Temple of Fire Baptized. Here he was indeed to be converted to his unknown father's faith and to reject the temptation of his stepfather's. As he hangs, suspended between heaven and hell, the first major voice he hears is the "malicious, ironic voice" of the devil, of his stepfather. It told him "to leave this temple and go out into the world . . . if he did not want to become like all the other niggers."

But when he rejects the devil's temptation to surrender his destiny to be a leader of his people, when he refuses to be exiled by his stepfather, "Then the darkness began to murmur—a terrible sound—and John's ears trembled. . . . This sound had filled John's life, so it now seemed, from the moment he had first drawn breath. . . . Yes, he had heard it all his life, but it was only now that his ears were opened to this sound that came from darkness . . . that yet bore each sure witness to the glory of the light. And now in his moaning . . . he heard it in himself—it rose from his bleeding, his cracked-open heart. . . . And he struggled to flee—out of this darkness, out of this company. . . . *Who are these?* Who are they? They were the despised and rejected, the wretched and the spat upon . . . and he was in their company. . . . And he began to shout for help, seeing before him the lash . . . seeing his head bowed down forever. . . . And a voice . . spoke to John. . . . Go through. . . . And a sweetness filled John as he heard this voice, and heard the song of singing. . . . He opened his eyes on the morning and found [the congregation] rejoicing for him. The trembling he had known

in the darkness had been the echo of their joyful feet—
their feet, bloodstained forever . . . they moved on the
bloody road forever. . . . No power could hold this army
back. . . . One day they would compel the earth to heave
upward, and surrender the waiting dead. . . . Yes, the night
had passed, the powers of darkness had been beaten back.
He moved among the saints. . . . The sun had come full
awake. It was waking the streets, and the houses, and cry-
ing at the windows . . . 'I'm ready,' John said, 'I'm coming. I'm on my way.'"

John, or James Baldwin, had joined the suffering
brotherhood of Negroes, and he would lead them to salvation, teaching them that they had no real burden of guilt
to distort their souls but were kept from happiness only
by the false teachings of a white society which had
rendered itself impotent by choosing civilization rather than
nature, inhibition rather than spontaneity, fear rather than
joy, and hate rather than love. Baldwin's second novel,
*Giovanni's Room*, is his slashing analysis of the impotence
of white America.

The hero of *Giovanni's Room* is David, the descendant of those white men who "conquered a continent, pushing across death-laden plains, until they came to an ocean
which faced away from Europe into a darker past." David
is the child of the vanquished Lost Generation. He is an
expatriate in Paris. He has fled from the United States
because he is running away from himself. "I had decided
to allow no room in the universe for something which
shamed and frightened me. I succeeded very well—by not
looking at myself, by remaining, in effect, in constant mo-
tion."

David has exiled himself from the New World because
he has looked into his own heart and has seen the depths
of darkness there. He can no longer stand the hypocrisy of
America which tries to sweep this darkness under the rug.
He has come to Paris where darkness is bought and sold

like every other commodity. Here, like the Parisians, he can
pretend that darkness has lost its terror when it has become merchandise. In other words, he is still trying to
preserve his American innocence. His continuing commitment to his national faith is revealed in his conversation
with the bartender, Giovanni.

"'I don't see why the world is so new for Americans,'
said Giovanni. 'After all, you are all merely emigrants. And
you did not leave Europe so very long ago.'

"'The ocean is very wide,' I said. 'We have led different lives than you. . . . Surely you can understand that
this would make us a very different people?'

"'Ah! If it had only made you a different people!' he
laughed. 'As though with enough time and all that fearful
energy and virtue you people have, everything will be
settled, solved, put in its place . . . all the serious, dreadful
things, like pain and death and love, in which you
Americans do not believe.' "

The irony of this conversation is that Giovanni is the
symbolic European whose ancestors came to America to
escape pain and death and love. His confrontation with
David is the confrontation of the European hope that
reality can be escaped in the New World with the living
denial of that hope. Desperately, Giovanni throws himself
into David's arms. This Old World man cannot save himself. He needs a savior from the New World. This is the
symbolism of Giovanni's room which was in complete dis-
order expressing Giovanni's grief and desire for punishment
and David "was to destroy this room and give to Giovanni
a new and better life. This life could only be my own,
which, in order to transform Giovanni's, must first become
a part of Giovanni's room."

While he loves Giovanni, he also hates him for bringing into the open his abnormality. He does not want to be
an outcast from society, to challenge its inhibitions, and
disregards a friend's warning that if "you play it safe long

enough . . . you'll end up trapped in your own dirty body, forever and forever and forever—like me." Unable to give Giovanni his complete commitment because he cannot accept his own homosexual instincts as natural and, therefore, good, David abandons his friend.

David, indeed, is revealed as doubly impotent, since he has also abandoned the "emancipated" American girl, Hella, to whom he had proposed marriage. Hella had come to realize that "I wasn't free, that I couldn't be free until I was attached—no, committed—to someone." But David was incapable of that violation of the self which was necessary for fruitful leadership. Hella must return to the United States knowing that she will continue to face an existence without meaning because David is like all American men, and "if women are supposed to be led by men and there aren't any men to lead them, what happens then?"

David is left in solitude as he seeks a way out of the prison of ideology, and his thoughts turn toward the acceptance of his body, toward the acceptance of that primitivism which can save him and the white world, Europe and America, from the inhibitions and the commercialization of civilization. "When I was a child, I spoke as a child, I understood as a child, I thought as a child: but when I became a man, I put away childish things. I long to make this prophecy come true. I look at my sex, my troubling sex and wonder how it can be redeemed. . . . The key to my salvation, which cannot save my body, is hidden in my flesh."

The implication of Baldwin's first two novels is that the primitive Negro who could accept suffering and deny guilt could save white America and white Europe from the burden of guilt imposed by the inhibitions of civilization. But his romantic primitivism is so extreme that it necessarily contradicts this framework of social salvation. He can posit no reality beyond the particular individual. For him, the abstract is artificial, the artificial is civilization, civilization is inhibition, inhibition is guilt, and the whole purpose of spiritual salvation for the individual is the transcendence of guilt. He must end with Norman Mailer in a theology of personal salvation which separates the particular saint from the sinful brotherhood of mankind. And if the Baldwin saint is not physically impotent, he is yet as sterile as Rojack and Natty Bumppo. This is the tragic impasse of Baldwin's most recent novel, *Another Country*.

He divides the story into three parts. Book One, "Easy Rider," deals with the white liberal who refuses to recognize the reality of suffering and the need to meet it with perfect love. Book Two, "Any Day Now," suggests the inevitable confrontation of the white liberal with the reality of suffering. And Book Three is "Toward Bethlehem," when the white liberal has been led to accept suffering with love as the human condition by the example of the Negro, Rufus, who has sacrificed himself to make possible the redemption of the world. But the only white liberal who has been called unto holiness by the crucifixion of Rufus is Eric, the white southerner who searched for love among "the warm, black people" and was rejected by Rufus. And the irony of this conclusion is so extreme that it becomes mockery when Eric's lover Yves arrives in the United States from France and strides "through the barriers, more high-hearted than he had ever been as a child, into that city which the people from heaven had made their home." He is striding, of course, into the arms of Eric. Together they are in Bethlehem, while the rest of Americans, white and black, continue to suffer in their alienation from their true selves, prisoners of the hypocritical codes of their bankrupt civilization. And Eric and Yves, in the perfect brotherly love of "another country," live in that sterile isolation from the sinful brotherhood of mankind which characterized the idyll of Deerslayer and Chingachgook.

It is interesting to note, in passing, that Baldwin's dream of national redemption by the crusading phalanx of Negro or white Negro saints would seem to be destroyed by the same unredeemable factor which frustrated Mailer's hope of social salvation—woman. Apparently women refuse to surrender their separate identities and reach perfect communion with the saints.

## 3

Norman Mailer has said that Saul Bellow lacks the apocalyptic vision. He is right in the sense that the mature Bellow of *Henderson the Rain King* and *Herzog* is stridently hostile to the tradition of romanticism in western civilization, which he sees as the disastrous source for the millennial ideal that has cursed modern times. But Mailer is wrong in the sense that each of Bellow's novels from the earliest, *Dangling Man* in 1944, to the most recent, *Herzog* in 1964, is concerned with the crisis in our national culture when the traditional faith in a utopian end to history begins to weaken and no longer persuades our hearts and minds.

Saul Bellow's novels, like those of Henry James more than a half-century before, are indeed concerned with the American apocalyptic imagination, and his purpose, too, is to destroy this tradition. His early works parallel those of James not only in that they reveal his sense of the bankruptcy of the myth of the American Adam, but also because they show that, while his intelligence had become critical of this tradition, his heart had not yet become free to find a new position of spiritual commitment. Each of his novels begins as destructive criticism and gradually becomes a pilgrimage toward a constructive goal until he too can finally take the golden bowl of civilization in his hands and accept with love the moral responsibility of holding its shattered halves, its unmendable dualisms, in a meaningful and worthwhile whole.

Bellow's first novel, *Dangling Man*, opens with a jour-

nal entry that marks the beginning of the chronicle of
his personal crisis within the framework of the national
crisis. "To keep a journal nowadays is considered a kind
of self-indulgence. . . . For this is an era of Hardboiledom.
. . . Most serious matters are closed to the hardboiled.
They are unpractical in introspection, and therefore badly
equipped to deal with opponents whom they cannot shoot
like big game or outdo in daring. If you have difficulties,
grapple with them silently, goes one of their command-
ments. To hell with that! I intend to talk about mine. . . .
In my present state of demoralization, it has become necessary for me to keep a journal." It is within the theater of
his own mind and heart, that the author will stage the
ideological conflict between the Eternal and the American
Adams.

Each of Bellow's six novels is the inner history of one
man dangling over the abyss of nothingness. The pit has
opened before Bellow and his fictional heroes because they,
as Americans, have reached maturity expecting perfection;
they carry the burden of innocence. Now they are confronted with the vision of a future in which there will be
no fulfillment of an earthly utopia. The garden path which
was supposed to lead to a New World has instead led to
this brink of nothingness. Such is the situation of Joseph,
the first of Bellow's dangling men.

Unable to communicate with other individuals, Joseph
debates with himself and records the conclusions in his
journal. "The most important experience of our time [is]
dying," he argues, and because of this, modern man has
become afraid of freedom. If man can no longer hope that
his actions will bring about a heavenly city on earth, what
new power, what new faith can renew his power to act?
Joseph believes that a return to traditional faith would be
the only means to restore meaning to the world, but he refuses to sacrifice his intelligence to what he considers the
demands of mystery. He will remain rational and impotent.

The final irony of his situation as neutral observer is that society refuses to allow him to stay in his room. He is drafted to serve its purposes. "I am no longer to be held accountable for myself; I am grateful for that. I am in other hands, relieved of self-determination, freedom cancelled.

"Hurray for regular hours!

"And for the supervision of the spirit!

"Long live regimentation!"

Bellows' second novel, *The Victim*, followed immediately after the war. Asa Leventhal, the "victim," is the average American who represents the other side of the coin of innocence which Joseph had described as "Hard-boiledom." Asa prizes security above all, and is angry because reality does not square with this dream. Holding a grudge against things as they are, he has withdrawn into the safety of the routine of his job and his marriage, the spiritual victim of his own frustrated expectations of a heaven on earth. Nevertheless, he considers himself the unwitting vicitim of a culture which teaches that love for one's neighbor is useless when love has lost its power to bring the millennium.

The logical culmination of Bellow's analysis of our society's sterility in the post-World War II era comes in his short novel, *Seize the Day*—a day in the life of Tommy Wilhelm, who learns that the promise of the American dream can be fulfilled only in death. Abandoned by the psychologist, Tamkin, who had promised him financial and emotional salvation, Tommy blunders into a mortuary to weep before Tamkin's corpse. Here is the peace he expected in life—the peace of the dead.

Is life worth living when the apocalyptic dream is destroyed? Can the modern American find the power to act when he no longer can think of himself as potentially a new man worthy of living in a New World Garden? In his first novel, Bellow could not answer yes. But the increasingly biting criticism of the position of the dangling man in *The Victim* and *Seize the Day* suggests that he, like Henry James before him, was illuminating every weakness of the myth of self-sufficient freedom in order to liberate his heart from its nostalgia for this bankrupt faith.

In *The Adventures of Augie March, Henderson the Rain King,* and *Herzog,* Bellow was to search for an alternative value to the state of nature—civilization.

Adventures abound for Augie March in his pursuit of freedom and perfection, but he comes to see that his life is just as unfree and sterile as his ambitious brother Simon's. Has he been wrong about viewing freedom as release from the imperfect brotherhood of man, and love as the way to transcend society rather than to accept it? Maybe the major conflict of life is not between society and the individual, but within the individual himself. "In yourself you labor, you wage combat, settle scores, remember insults, fight, reply, deny, blab, denounce, triumph, outwit, overcome, vindicate, cry, persist, absolve, die, and rise again. All by yourself! Where is everybody? Inside your breast and skin, the entire cast."

In the end, Augie March is still alienated from his fellow men, still an exile—another dangling man. But at least he has followed his pilgrimage in search of perfect love to the clearcut realization of the bankruptcy of this ideal; intellectually he has grasped the inadequacy of this false faith. His heart was reaching out for identification with his imperfect fellow man with whom he had been raised in suffering and in joy. Only one more step and he would cease to be a dangling man. He could come home and feel himself committed to mankind as it existed, to the eternal Adam of the human condition.

Much of the brilliance of Bellow's metaphysical novels comes from his mastery of detail. In the tradition of James, his symbolic characters lived in a world of realistic dialogue and manners. It was possible for critics to look at his first four novels and deny their philosophical burden, while praising the author for the insight and depth of his depiction of the American-Jewish experience. To clear away any confusion about the relationship of his personal pilgrimage to the national culture, Bellow was now ready to affirm the worth of sinful man, to posit the salvation of the dangling man in terms of an obvious national allegory. The hero of *Henderson the Rain King* is a member of the old American aristocracy, the legitimate heir of the Washingtons and Adamses.

The privileged, affluent Henderson is a frustrated Gulliver, haunted by a voice within him that cries, "I want, I want, I want," yet never says what is wanted. Henderson's curse was the hope of perfection—"I wanted to raise myself into another world. My life and deeds were a prison." And when the hope failed he was left suspended over the abyss of nothingness. If his America refused to become the New World Garden, he would use his ancestral estate to raise pigs.

But still the voice pursues him, and he flees to an unexplored region in Africa. Perhaps there, among the peaceful Arnewi who worship their cows, he can find tranquility. But these good people are dying because of the drought; they have a body of water but they will not drink of it because it is filled with frogs. Henderson, the crusading American, manages to kill the frogs—and destroy the entire water supply.

Still the crusader, he moves on to the warlike Wariri tribe who worship the lion instead of the cow. The Wariri are ruled by a king who has been educated in the outside world and is certain that human nature can be changed; he plans to end human weakness by making men as brave as lions. When the king is killed by a lion, the Wariri would make Henderson their ruler, but he escapes and returns home, a wiser if not particularly sadder man.

He has seen the folly of humans who try to be animals

rather than men. The quest for perfection and innocence can only destroy the humanity of man and reduce him to the level of a non-human monster. No longer will Henderson attempt to be a rain king in America, seeking the miracle which will make Americans as tranquil as cows and as brave as lions. Joyfully, he will accept his humanity and his brotherhood with men in society, knowing that neither he nor they are damned because of their weaknesses. Now that he has found himself, he can love people and not pigs. He has escaped the prophecy of Daniel by rediscovering the meaning of the phrase, "The forgiveness of sins is perpetual and righteousness first is not required."

Having diagnosed the sickness of American society and discovered the remedy, Bellow was ready to accept the responsibility for the ancient injunction—Physician, heal thyself. From the national allegory of *Henderson the Rain King,* he turns to the personal history of Moses Herzog, to record the liberation of a particular individual from bondage.

In 1964, some twenty years after the publication of the journal of his first dangling man, Bellow presented the innermost thoughts of a man who was much like Joseph. Moses Herzog had written his Ph.D. dissertation on "The State of Nature in Seventeenth and Eighteenth Century English and French Political Philosophy," had become a professor and had published a book, "Romanticism and Christianity." Nevertheless, his life had fallen apart; he had lost his power to lead an ordered existence.

Desperately, Herzog searches back through his history for the perspective which will help him to act purposefully once again. He remembers his father's anger because "in his father's eyes [he was] stubbornly unEuropean, that is, innocent by deliberate choice. Moses refused to know evil. But he could not refuse to experience it."

This had been the source of his tragedy. Intellectually, he had early recognized that there was weakness in romanticism; his dissertation and his book had been criticisms of romanticism. In an abstract way, he knew that the romantic emphasis on the self was misleading and had caused major problems in modern civilization. But as a young man, he had thought of himself as Joseph, the favored son, and his dreams of omnipotence had set him above other men. Now Moses saw that in his actual life he had sold himself into bondage to romanticism. With sardonic humor, he looks back at this life of lies and sees the contradiction between his head and his heart. Only now, when his romanticism is finally purged, can he stop writing letters to the world to explain his troubles. An intellectual, he has at last escaped "the chief ambiguity that afflicts intellectuals, and this is that civilized individuals hate and resent the civilization that makes their lives possible. What they love is an imaginary human situation invented by their own genius and which they believe is the only true and only human reality."

Disappointed in their millennialism, Herzog thought, many intellectuals have reacted by denying the existence of any ideals. "This generation thinks . . . that nothing faithful, vulnerable, fragile can be durable or have any true power." He rejects these polar alternatives of a heaven on earth or nothingness, of total happiness or total suffering. The romantic choice between the American Adam and the dangling man is an illusion. The individual is always part of a community and therefore "brotherhood is what makes a man human. If I owe God a human life, this is where I fall down. 'Man liveth not by Self alone but in his brother's face. . . . Each shall behold the Eternal Father and love and joy abound.' When the preachers of dread tell you that others only distract you from metaphysical freedom then you must turn away from them. The real and essential question is one of our employment by other human beings and their employment by us. Without this true employment you never dread death, you cultivate it.

And consciousness when it doesn't clearly understand what to live for, what to die for, can only abuse and ridicule itself. . . . A man doesn't need happiness for *himself*. No, he can put up with any amount of torment. . . . this is the unwritten history of man . . . his power to do without gratification for himself provided there is something great, something into which his being, and all beings, can go." For Herzog, that something was responsible membership in the sinful brotherhood of mankind. This is "the question of ordinary human experience. . . . The strength of a man's virtue or spiritual capacity measured by his ordinary life."

Moses Herzog has achieved a new power to act creatively and constructively because, unlike the young man, Joseph, he will accept the mystery of life. "But what do you want, Herzog," he asks himself. "But that's just it—not a solitary thing. I am pretty well satisfied to be, to be just as it is willed, and for as long as I may remain in occupancy." For Herzog, however, this is now a lesser mystery than Joseph's dream of intellectual omnipotence, "the delusion of total explanations."

Fully alive for perhaps the first time, Herzog falls in love with his old house in the Berkshires. He enjoys the air, the sky, the trees, the flowers, the birds. He takes to his heart all these symbols of immediate life and the house itself as a symbol of life expressed through time. No longer demanding perfection that transcends immediate experience, he is young again, perceiving all things with the simple appreciation of a child. He has learned at last that one can accept happiness without guilt if one does not worship at the romantic shrine dedicated to nothing but the pursuit of happiness.

# Epilogue

And so we come to the end of our story that deals with the metaphysical concern of the American novelist from James Fenimore Cooper to Saul Bellow. No important American novelist has been able to escape a direct confrontation with the American dream. The first European pioneers so firmly defined the meaning of the New World as the Garden in which men of the Old World would be redeemed that their descendants have not yet been able to find another meaning for their social experience. In spite of the warnings of Cooper, Hawthorne, Melville, James and, most recently, Bellow, that this is an impossible enterprise which twists the heart, blights the mind, and results in social sterility, most American intellectuals have chosen to remain loyal to this antique faith. They have chosen with Fitzgerald to "beat on, boats against the current, borne back ceaselessly into the past."

There are signs, however, that this stubborn refusal to escape from bondage to romanticism may be weakening in this second half of the twentieth century. It is not the exodus of Moses Herzog alone which can be used as evidence for such an assertion; after all, Cooper also attempted to end the existence of the dangling man.

In the grim stoicism of Cozzens and the hysterical affirmations of Mailer and Baldwin we can see intimations of crumbling and disintegration in the wall of faith that has sustained belief in the ultimate fulfillment of the American Garden. Only time will tell if the pilgrimage of Moses Herzog away from the promised land of the chosen people toward the civilization of the sinful brotherhood of mankind does indeed symbolize a major turning point in our national cultural history.